I0753307

BEYOND DISPLACEMENT

RECLAIMING HUMAN DIGNITY

HUMAN RIGHTS REALITIES AND PATHWAYS TO RECOVERY AMONG IDPS IN NIGERIA, CAMEROON AND SOUTH AFRICA.

PAUL NKEMNGU ACHA-ANYI

Published by Acha-Anyi Academic Press
Saint Paul, Minnesota, 55112, United States of America.

ISBN 979-8-99577-000-8

The following excerpts from the Holy Father resonate throughout this book:

"Behind the statistics [of displacement] are faces, stories, shattered hopes. …

The world thirsts for peace. Enough of wars, with their painful toll of death, destruction, and exile. …

Security is a priority, but it must always be exercised with respect for human rights, combining rigor and compassion, with particular attention to the most vulnerable."

—Pope Leo XIV, Cameroon, April 15, 2026

ABOUT THE AUTHOR

Paul Nkemngu Acha-Anyi is a professor in the Department of Tourism and Hospitality Management at Walter Sisulu University in the Eastern Cape Province of South Africa. Paul is an award-winning, NRF-rated social science researcher with over twenty-one years of experience. His research focuses on the sustainable development of communities, with particular emphasis on tourism, human rights, and the socio-economic resilience of vulnerable populations, such as internally displaced persons.

Professor Acha-Anyi has authored and edited three academic books titled *Introduction to tourism planning and Development: igniting Africa's tourism economy* (Acha-Anyi, 2018), *Fundamentals of tourism: an African perspective* (Acha-Anyi, 2020), and *Project management for the service sector* (Acha-Anyi, 2021). He has published over sixty-three papers in international journals and has supervised the theses of over 260 postgraduate students at doctoral, master's, and honors degree levels. Some of his grant-funded continental research projects include studies on the impacts of hosting the AFCON finals on communities in Cameroon, human rights among internally displaced persons (IDPs) in Cameroon, South Africa, and Nigeria, and the effects of climate change on tourism-reliant communities in Tanzania, Kenya, and Rwanda.

PREFACE

Internal displacement has emerged as one of the most pressing yet insufficiently understood human rights challenges of our time. Across the globe—and particularly in Sub-Saharan Africa—millions of individuals are forced to flee their homes due to conflict, environmental disasters, and insecurity, yet remain within the borders of their own countries. Unlike refugees, internally displaced persons (IDPs) often fall into a protection gap: they are legally citizens, but practically marginalized, navigating fragile systems that frequently fail to guarantee their rights, dignity, and well-being.

This book contributes to ongoing debates on internal displacement by advancing a central argument: that internal displacement is not merely a humanitarian condition, but a multidimensional and systemic human rights crisis. While existing scholarship has made significant contributions—particularly in documenting the scale, causes, and immediate needs of displaced populations, much of this work has tended to treat displacement as an emergency phenomenon requiring short-term humanitarian responses. In contrast, this manuscript situates internal displacement within a broader human rights, structural, and developmental framework, emphasizing long-term patterns of inequality, governance deficits, and institutional failure.

A key component of this book is its comparative and multi-contextual approach. By examining three distinct national contexts—Cameroon, South Africa, and Nigeria—it captures the diversity of displacement experiences across Africa while identifying shared structural drivers. Cameroon illustrates conflict-driven displacement rooted in political marginalization; South Africa highlights climate-induced and socio-economic displacement in an urbanizing society; and Nigeria demonstrates the complex interplay between violence, organized crime, and ethno-religious tensions. This comparative design enables the book to move beyond single-case analysis and offers a holistic understanding of displacement across different typologies—conflict, climate, and crime.

Another distinctive feature of this manuscript is its integration of multiple theoretical frameworks, including the rights-based approach, the capability approach, human security, and African communitarian perspectives. By combining these frameworks, the book provides a nuanced understanding of displacement that goes beyond legal entitlements to consider lived realities, social relationships, and structural inequalities. In particular, the inclusion of Africa-centered perspectives, such as communitarian ethics and postcolonial critiques, addresses a gap in existing literature, which has often been dominated by Eurocentric paradigms.

Methodologically, the book makes an important contribution through its mixed-methods design, combining quantitative survey data with qualitative narratives from internally displaced persons themselves. This dual approach allows for both generalizable insights and deep contextual understanding. Importantly, it amplifies the voices of IDPs—many of whom live outside formal camps and are frequently overlooked in research—thereby addressing a critical gap identified in previous studies.

The findings presented in this manuscript challenge several assumptions in existing literature. First, they demonstrate that human rights among IDPs are deeply interconnected, with deficits in one domain—such as economic security—undermining others, including civic participation and personal safety. Second, they reveal that displacement experiences are not uniform, but are shaped by intersectional factors, such as gender, age, education, and employment status. Third, they show that even in contexts with strong legal frameworks, such as South Africa, structural inequalities and implementation gaps continue to limit the realization of rights.

In contrast to many previous works that focus primarily on either legal frameworks or humanitarian interventions, this book adopts a comprehensive, interdisciplinary perspective that bridges theory, empirical evidence, and policy. It not only diagnoses the problem but also proposes practical, rights-based policy solutions, making it relevant to scholars, policymakers, development practitioners, and humanitarian actors.

Ultimately, this manuscript seeks to shift the discourse from one of crisis management to one of structural transformation. It argues that addressing internal displacement requires more than temporary relief; it demands sustained efforts to tackle the root causes of inequality, insecurity, and marginalization. By foregrounding the human rights realities of internally displaced persons, this book aims to contribute to more inclusive, just, and sustainable approaches to displacement in Africa and beyond.

OVERVIEW - A WORLD ON THE MOVE

Imagine a world where millions of people are uprooted from their homes, not by choice, but by the relentless forces of conflict, violent crime, and disaster. This is the reality for at least 124 million (one in every sixty-seven) people today, as families embark on perilous journeys in search of basic human rights provisions, such as the right to life, access to potable water, food, and safety. While some displaced people find refuge within their native countries, becoming internally displaced persons (IDPs), others flee across borders, earning the title of refugees. Understanding the distinction between IDPs and refugees is crucial, as it delineates responsibility and shapes the support and protection these individuals receive. This book goes beyond theory to offer readers a rare glimpse into the daily challenges faced by internally displaced persons in selected Sub-Saharan African countries. While the first chapter shapes the discourse on the meaning and scale of internal displacement, the second chapter examines the historical and religious context to illustrate the protracted nature of the internal displacement crisis. The third chapter explores international frameworks that have been developed to address the crisis of internal displacement while the three subsequent chapters, (four, five and six) provide the reader with empirical information captured from participating IDPs about their experiences as they fled from the Anglophone crisis in Cameroon, the high levels of organized criminality in Nigeria, or the flooding and xenophobic tensions in the provinces of KwaZulu-Natal and Western Cape in South Africa. The goal in sifting through this first-hand data is to give the reader a comprehensive understanding of the impacts of internal displacement in the affected countries, to stimulate reflection on the situation of IDPs, and to engender policy and implementation shifts that could mitigate the plight of affected people and communities. Chapter seven presents a comparative analysis of empirical data from the three countries, highlighting key differences and similarities based on the experiences of IDPs. The final chapter summarizes avenues for support and protection for people caught up in the unfortunate situation of internal displacement.

TABLE OF CONTENTS

CHAPTER 1

Human Displacement: Concept, Context, and Scope

Abstract

This chapter provides a comprehensive foundation for understanding internal displacement, examining its concept, causes, and impacts, particularly within Sub-Saharan Africa. Despite its scale, the plight of internally displaced persons (IDPs) remains under-recognized due to their location within national borders and the absence of consistent visibility and protection.

By clarifying key concepts and situating internal displacement within broader socio-political realities, this chapter establishes the analytical groundwork for the book. It also outlines the mixed-methods approach used to collect empirical data from IDPs in Cameroon, Nigeria, and South Africa.

Keywords: internal displacement, Sub-Saharan Africa, human rights, conflict, vulnerability

1.1 Introduction

Across the world, millions of people are forced to leave their homes due to conflict, disasters, and insecurity. While some cross international borders and become refugees, many remain within their countries of origin. These individuals, known as internally displaced persons (IDPs), often experience profound vulnerability and limited protection (Internal Displacement Monitoring Center [IDMC], 2024).

Unlike refugees, who benefit from international protection regimes, IDPs remain under the jurisdiction of their own governments. This often results in gaps in protection, visibility, and assistance (United Nations [UN], 1998). As a result, internal displacement represents a critical yet underexplored human rights challenge.

This chapter introduces the concept of internal displacement, explores its causes and impacts, and outlines the methodological framework guiding this study of IDPs in Cameroon, Nigeria, and South Africa.

1.2 Understanding Internal Displacement

The concept of internal displacement has evolved over time, particularly in relation to its distinction from refugee movements. Early scholarship often conflated internally displaced persons with refugees, leading to conceptual ambiguity in policy and practice (Cohen & Deng, 1998).

The United Nations Guiding Principles on Internal Displacement define IDPs as:

"Persons or groups of persons who have been forced or obliged to flee or to leave their homes . . . and who have not crossed an internationally recognized State border" (UN, 1998, p. 5).

This definition highlights four defining characteristics:

1. Forced or involuntary movement.
2. Internal relocation within national borders.
3. Multiple causes (conflict, disasters, human rights violations).
4. Continued need for protection and assistance.

Unlike refugees, IDPs are not covered by a single binding international convention, making their protection more dependent on national governments and broader human rights frameworks (Kälin, 2008).

1.3 Internal Displacement in Sub-Saharan Africa

Sub-Saharan Africa remains one of the most affected regions globally, accounting for a significant proportion of internally displaced populations (IDMC, 2024). Countries such as Sudan, the Democratic Republic of Congo, Somalia, Ethiopia, and Nigeria host millions of IDPs due to conflict and instability.

In Cameroon, internal displacement is driven primarily by the Anglophone crisis, while in South Africa, environmental disasters, such as floods, play a significant role. Nigeria presents a complex case where displacement results from insurgency, communal conflict, and criminal violence.

These patterns illustrate that internal displacement in Africa is shaped by multiple and intersecting drivers, including conflict, climate change, and socio-economic inequality (African Union, 2019).

1.4 Causes of Internal Displacement

1.4.1 Conflict and Violence

Armed conflict remains the leading cause of internal displacement globally. Civil wars, insurgencies, and communal violence force populations to flee in search of safety (IDMC, 2024).

In the African contexts, these conflicts are further intensified by ethnic, religious, and political tensions. According to the Stockholm International Peace Research Institute (SIPRI), eighteen countries in Sub-Saharan Africa were embroiled in armed conflicts in 2022 (SIPRI,

2024). Even more worrying is the assertion by DefenceWeb (2024) that the Sub-Saharan African region experienced more armed conflicts in 2023 than any other region in the world. Some of the countries affected by armed conflict in Sub-Saharan Africa are the Democratic Republic of Congo (DRC), Sudan, the Central African Republic (CAR), Nigeria, Cameroon, and Mozambique. These unrelenting armed conflicts are responsible for most displacements in the region.

Sadly, wars and insurgencies are not the only forms of violence causing people to abandon their homes in search of safer places. Communal violence in Nigeria and South Sudan has also displaced many people. Generally motivated by ethnic, religious, or other reasons, communities unleash violent attacks on other groups of people, causing vulnerable people to flee to safer places.

Uncontrolled criminality that authorities have failed to restrain or even contain has also resulted in the displacement of some people who want to raise their families, especially children, in more conducive environments. The abduction of children from schools and businesspeople for ransom has been reported in many countries in Sub-Saharan Africa. Political violence is often orchestrated by oppressive leaders who are eager to silence dissenting opinions, cause repression, and inflict terror on political opponents. Regardless of its trigger, violence makes people feel unsafe and seek shelter.

1.4.2 Climate and Environmental Factors

Climate change is increasingly recognized as a major driver of displacement. Floods, droughts, and other environmental hazards disproportionately affect vulnerable communities (Intergovernmental Panel on Climate Change [IPCC], 2022).

In Sub-Saharan Africa, weak infrastructure and limited adaptive capacity exacerbate the impact of environmental disasters. The increasing frequency and severity of environmental disasters are putting the lives of many individuals and communities at risk, and Sub-Saharan Africa has borne its share of the brunt. In fact, reports indicate that seven out of the ten most vulnerable countries to climate change are in Sub-Saharan Africa, with Chad occupying the unenviable first position, followed by Somalia, the Democratic Republic of Congo (DRC), the Central African Republic (CAR), Nigeria, Ethiopia, and South Sudan (IBERDROLA, 2024). Not only have occurrences of events such as drought, tornadoes, floods, cyclones, and rainstorms become more difficult to predict, but they have also increased in intensity. Available data suggest that 1,436 disaster events were recorded in twenty-nine African countries between 2000 and 2023, with 66% triggered by floods, 15.4% by storms, and 17.7% by droughts (Africa Risk Capacity, 2024). These disaster events have exerted a huge toll on human life, affecting more than ten million people, causing about 17000 fatalities, and destroying livelihoods.

1.4.3 Human Rights Violations

Human rights abuses—including forced evictions, violence, and persecution—continue to displace populations. In many cases, civilians are caught between state and non-state actors, with limited protection (Amnesty International, 2022). In its resolution, ACHPR. Res.582 (LXXVIII) of 2024, The African Commission on Human and Peoples' Rights (the African Commission) lamented the high level of human rights abuses such as abductions, arbitrary executions, extortion, gender-based violence, etc., and the precarious living conditions that have forced many people out of their homes and fueled the over sixteen million internally displaced persons on the continent (ACHPR, 2024). The many armed conflicts and high levels of criminality and violence have exacerbated these human rights abuses. Some examples of countries in Sub-Saharan Africa where human rights abuses have exacerbated internal displacement include Sudan, Ethiopia, the Democratic Republic of Congo, Nigeria, and Cameroon. Fighting between the Sudanese Armed Forces (SAF) and the Rapid Support Forces (RSF) has resulted in the indiscriminate targeting and bombing of the civilian population, forcing about 10.7 million people to be displaced internally (Office for the Coordination of Humanitarian Affairs, 2024). Human rights abuses have also prompted the displacement of many people in countries such as Ethiopia, the DRC, and Cameroon, where civilians have been caught in the crossfire between government forces and armed dissident groups. In Nigeria, Boko Haram and other armed groups have abducted, maimed, and killed several people, thereby forcing many others to flee from their homes.

1.4.4 Development-Induced Displacement

Large-scale development projects, such as dams and urban expansion, can lead to displacement when communities are relocated without adequate compensation or planning (Cernea, 2000). Commonly referred to as development projects, activities associated with urban renewal, mining operations, and the building of dams have often triggered the displacement of many people through the destruction of their livelihoods, social networks, homes, or communities. While these projects might result in huge capital injections and growth in the local economy, they hardly improve the living conditions of residents or the development conditions in the area. However, the debate on the responsibilities of project developers and development agencies regarding human rights law has been going on for some time. Critics argue that funding agencies such as the World Bank ought to do more to compel development organizations to whom they lend money to respect the human rights of the people their projects displace and remedy or mitigate the damage development projects inflict on the environment (Alston et al., 2014). Others further argue that as a funding institution, the World Bank has a legal obligation to incorporate human rights law into its operating framework, without which the bank would be missing an opportunity to foster the course of human rights around the world (Sarfaty, 2012).

Unfortunately, this view is not held by all. While agreeing with the view that development agencies should be mindful of the impacts of the projects they undertake on the well-being of vulnerable people, Posner (2016) argues that using human rights law as a basis for assessing the value of projects would not be helpful, primarily because the subject of human rights is ambiguous, contentious, and politically charged. He concludes that there is little evidence to suggest that attempts to promote human rights using NGOs and other development organizations would be successful. The responsibility of enforcing human rights prescripts should be the responsibility of state governments or the ruling authorities.

Table 1.1 Examples of development projects in Sub-Saharan Africa that have resulted in internal displacement.

Name of project and location	**Purpose**	**Unintended impacts**
Gilgel Gibe III Dam in Omo River, Ethiopia.	A hydroelectric power plant costing about US$1.8 billion.	The dam has significantly altered the river's flow, affecting the livelihoods of those who depend on it for farming and fishing.
Lamu Port-South Sudan-Ethiopia Transport (LAPSSET) Corridor project in Kenya.	Plan, coordinate and manage the implementation of Lamu Port.	Displacement of local communities.
Bujagali Hydropower Project on the Nile River, Uganda.	The project aimed to increase electricity generation.	Displaced numerous communities. It also led to the relocation of people living in the project area.
Eko Atlantic City project in Lagos, Nigeria.	Urban development project aims to create a new city on reclaimed land.	Caused displacement of coastal communities. has displaced many residents in the process.

The diversity in the nature and motives of these development projects is worth noting. While the projects mentioned above are large-scale, it is important to note that people are also displaced by small-scale projects. Additionally, the controversy surrounding the cost-benefit analyses of development projects is ongoing. A lingering unanswered question is, "Does the rationale of the economic benefits derived from these projects suffice against the displacement that ensues?"

1.5 Impacts of Internal Displacement

Internal displacement has profound and multidimensional consequences:

- Health impacts: Increased exposure to disease, trauma, and mental health challenges.
- Security risks: Vulnerability to violence and exploitation.
- Economic disruption: Loss of livelihoods and increased poverty.
- Social fragmentation: Breakdown of family and community networks.
- Long-term vulnerability: Protracted displacement and limited recovery opportunities.

The impacts of internal displacement are not only wide-ranging but also life-changing for affected individuals and their families. Internally displaced persons usually flee from their homes at short notice, making it difficult for them to carry any life-sustaining items such as food, water, and medication. Some frequently mentioned impacts of internal displacement are discussed below:

1.5.1 Health and Well-Being

Research on the phenomenon of internal displacement has been described as quite limited in scope (Cantor, 2022). However, Swartz et al. (2023) acknowledge that within the body of literature exploring the experiences of internally displaced persons, health and wellness have received significant attention. The abrupt and unplanned nature of internal displacement creates conditions that increase the vulnerability of affected people to health and wellness challenges.

In their study on mental health and conflict in Nigeria, Adesina et al. (2020) observed that there is a high prevalence of mental health conditions such as post-traumatic stress disorders (PTSD), anxiety disorder, depression, substance misuse, psychosis, anti-social behaviors, somatic symptoms such as headaches, non-specific pains or discomfort in torso and limbs, dizziness, weakness, and fatigue among internally displaced persons.

1.5.2 Security and Protection

The immediate consequence of displacement is the loss of the security and protection afforded by the home, family, and immediate community. Living in unfamiliar surroundings leaves internally displaced persons quite vulnerable to acts of criminality and insecurity. In fact, the prevalence of gender-based violence among internally displaced persons has been widely documented in literature with notable contributions by Dahie et al., (2023) on the situation in IDP camps, Mogadishu-Somalia, Keralem Workie et al., (2024) detailing the plight among internally displaced women in Northwest Ethiopia, Umar et al., (2023) on the context of IDPs in Yobe State located in the North East of Nigeria and Boeyink et al., (2022) in Garowe and Kismayo in Somalia and South Kivu in the Democratic Republic of Congo (DRC). However, the security concerns of IDPs are not limited to protection from physical harm but equally extend to the need for food security, employment, and healthcare. Alleviating these concerns and protecting IDPs against individuals and groups trying to exploit any vulnerabilities is crucial to their welfare.

1.5.3 Mental Health and Psychological Well-Being

- A 2025 systematic review and meta-analysis on depressive symptoms among IDPs in Sub-Saharan Africa by Girum Nakie et al. (2025) finds a high prevalence of depression among displaced populations.
- Key risk factors consistently associated with depression include, low educational status, unemployment after displacement, loss or damage to property, physical illness, lack of basic needs (food, shelter, water), injury, loss of family/friends, and persistent instability.
- A separate meta-analysis (Tura Koshe et al., 2023) highlights alarmingly high prevalence of post-traumatic stress disorder (PTSD) among IDPs in Africa, with a wide range across studies (from ~12% to as high as 85%, depending on context.
- Persistent displacement, repeated exposure to trauma (violence, loss, forced flight), and poor living conditions (overcrowding, insecurity) are identified as major contributors to long-term mental health burdens.

Implication: Internal displacement is not just a physical/housing issue; it is a profound mental health crisis, with many IDPs at high risk of depression, PTSD, and psychosocial distress.

1.5.4 Health, Mortality, and Access to Services

- Displacement significantly undermines physical health and access to healthcare. A recent cross-sectional study among IDPs in camp-like settings in Sudan's White Nile State

(2023) documented high rates of both physical and mental health problems among displaced populations (Ali et al., 2024).

- A study by Yahaya et al. (2025) found that in many contexts, IDPs face deteriorated sanitary conditions, overcrowding, poor nutrition, risk of communicable diseases, inadequate maternal and child health services, and lack of continuity of care. For some, non-communicable diseases worsen due to disrupted care.
- The breakdown of health management systems, fragmentation of services, inadequate financing, and weak coordination among agencies compound morbidity and mortality risks among IDPs, especially in protracted displacement settings.

Implication: Displacement undermines basic rights to health and life; long-term neglect of health needs among IDPs can become a chronic public health burden.

1.5.5 Livelihoods, Economic Vulnerability, and Food Security

- The Internal Displacement Monitoring Center (IDMC, 2025) states that displacement disrupts livelihoods: loss of land, property, and farms, interruption of economic activities, loss of jobs, and breakdown of social networks that previously supported livelihoods. Analyses highlight that many IDPs, even when they find refuge, live in precarity, often dependent on aid or informal, precarious jobs.
- A growing share of displacement in Africa is climate- or disaster-induced (droughts, floods, cyclones). For example,

a 2024 study (Mateko & Vutula, 2024) found that natural disasters triggered massive relocations and strained urban and rural systems across multiple countries.

- Disaster-induced displacement often leads to overburdened urban/rural host communities, pressure on resources (water, land, housing), and environmental degradation, creating new cycles of vulnerability and poverty.
- In host communities (when IDPs are absorbed among existing populations), there are often economic stresses: competition over jobs, services, and resources, rising living costs, and social tensions, which complicate both humanitarian response and long-term development.

Implication: Internal displacement undermines economic stability and livelihoods in the short and long term. Recovery without sustainable livelihood restoration is unlikely, leaving many in chronic poverty and dependency.

1.5.6 Social Fabric, Community Disruption, and Social Networks

- Displacement fractures social networks, traditional support systems, and community cohesion. In many IDP contexts, people lose not only homes but also their extended community bonds, social capital, and customary support, which are often critical for survival and resilience.
- Children and youth in displacement suffer disrupted education, interrupted schooling, and loss of normal developmental environments, which have long-term implications for human capital, social mobility, and intergenerational inequality. While much data comes from older

reports, new analyses continue to flag education disruption as a core impact (IDMC, 2025).

- According to Tadesse et al. (2024), gender-based violence (GBV) emerges as a serious concern among displaced women and girls. Tadesse et al. (2024) GBV among refugees and internally displaced women across Africa shows elevated prevalence, driven by factors like instability, loss of protection, breakdown of social norms, and lack of security in camps or displacement settings.
- Social integration in host communities is often hampered; host populations may resent or stigmatize IDPs. This can generate long-term marginalization, exclusion from services or livelihood opportunities, and social conflict between host and displaced populations.

Implication: Internal displacement not only displaces individuals physically but also erodes social cohesion, disrupts intergenerational inheritance of social capital, and can entrench social exclusion and vulnerability, especially for women, children, and other vulnerable groups. These impacts highlight the need for integrated and rights-based responses.

1.6 Methodological Approach

This book used a two-phase research design. The first phase was an extensive review of the literature on the concept and current situation of internal displacement, while the second consisted of empirical data collection and analysis. The outcome of this approach is evident in the split into four chapters reporting the findings of the literature review and four chapters detailing the results of the data collected from the IDPs. The following sections describe the study sites and explain the procedural aspects of the data collection.

Study Sites

The countries selected for this study were purposively identified to reflect the diverse causes of internal displacement and regional geopolitical differences. Hence, Cameroon was selected from the Economic Community of Central African States (CEMAC), with political instability as the main cause of internal displacement, Nigeria from the Economic Community of West African States (ECOWAS), with crime and ethnic tensions as the root causes of displacement (IDMC, 2024; Anierobi et al., 2024; Nnabuihe, 2020); and South Africa from the Southern African Development Community (SADC), with climate change and social tensions fueling internal displacement (IDMC, 2024, p. 34).

The design of this study was predicated on two key considerations of the problem, namely, the fact that the phenomenon of internal displacement is deeply entrenched in Sub-Saharan Africa (IDMC, 2024) and the personal and sensitive nature of the subject of human rights. This necessitated that a quantitative research approach be followed to delineate empirical aspects by factoring in the views of as many internally displaced persons as possible, while simultaneously adopting the qualitative design in order to benefit from the interpretative insights gathered through interviews with leading figures such as family heads and people responsible for general services such as security and administration. A multiple-case study design was also deemed appropriate, given the widespread nature of internal displacement in the region and the diverse causes, some man-made (wars, social unrest, communal conflicts, crime, etc.) and others nature-induced (floods, tornadoes, drought, etc.).

The population of this study consisted of internally displaced persons in the three countries identified (Cameroon, Nigeria, and South Africa). With reference to Cameroon, the International Organization for Migration (IOM) estimates the number of people displaced by the Anglophone crisis at 562,807 (IOM, 2022). The Northwest region had 231,281, the Southwest region 137,461, and the Littoral region 95,677 (IOM, 2022). Since this study was conducted across those three regions, the study population was estimated at 464,419.

Similarly, the study population in South Africa was considered to comprise 40,000 people displaced by floods in KwaZulu-Natal (UNICEF, 2023) and 200 people displaced by fires in the Western Cape province (Bredeveldt, 2023). The Internal Displacement Monitoring Center reports that the number of people displaced internally due to conflict and violence in Nigeria is about 3.3 million (IDMC, 2024. p. 31).

Krejcie and Morgan's (1970) sample size table was used as the validation tool for the sample in this study. Since the study populations exceeded 100,000 in the three case studies, sample sizes of 384 or more were considered valid (Krejcie & Morgan, 1970).

There are a few observations regarding the populations that are worth noting here. The first is that the population of IDPs in any community is relatively unstable because IDPs move in and out of the community as conditions improve either in their community of permanent residence or elsewhere. Secondly, even though IDPs live alongside community members, they are easily identifiable because community members usually offer them assistance to settle, especially in the case of families or people with children. Given this scenario, respondents in this study were sampled using simple random convenience sampling and occasional snowballing, as some IDPs voluntarily pointed out other IDPs to the field worker. This pattern of sampling and data collection from consenting IDPs was followed until the field workers reached saturation in each community they visited.

The data collection process started in Cameroon, and identifying IDPs was relatively easy because they live in groups. However, eleven community members were wrongly identified as IDPs since their houses were quite close to those of the IDPs. Once these people identified themselves as permanent residents, the invitation to participate in the study was withdrawn. On the other hand, correctly identified IDPs were approached and asked if they would agree to take part in the study. IDPs who gave their consent were handed a copy of the questionnaire to complete if they could read and write in English. Respondents who could not read or write in English had the questionnaire read to them and explained by the enumerator, who then marked the responses chosen by the respondent. Despite the invitation extended to all available IDPs to participate in the study, about 100 declined, generally citing a need to rush to complete their chores. It is also important to note that twenty-two potential respondents were politely refused participation in the study because they did not meet the minimum age of eighteen years. At the end of the data collection exercise, 577 completed questionnaires were collected from the respondents. After checking the collected questionnaires, forty-seven were found to be unusable because some were not fully completed, and others had multiple ticks on some questions. Thus, 530 questionnaires were retained as fully completed, with no multiple responses to the same question.

Research Instrument

In line with the quantitative design adopted in this study, a questionnaire was developed to serve as the data collection instrument. This survey instrument was divided into three sections. Section A focused on gathering demographic information to answer the first research question, aimed at understanding the profile of the IDPs. Section B explored respondents' perceptions of the extent to which various aspects of their human rights are met. Section C gathered data on the IDPs' motivations and aspirations regarding the human rights needs they most desire to see met. Questions on the human rights section of the questionnaire were mostly informed by the AU Convention for the Protection and Assistance of Internally Displaced Persons in Africa (Kampala Convention) (AU, 2012), the United Nations Declaration of Human Rights (UDHR) (UN, 1948) and *Human Rights Indicators: A Guide to Measurement and Implementation* (Office of the High Commissioner for Human Rights (OHCHR, 2021).

The research instrument had to be tested for validity, reliability, consistency, and clarity. In this regard, twenty IDPs in Durban, South Africa, were invited to complete the questionnaire. Results of the pilot study revealed a few ambiguities in some questions, which were addressed immediately. For example, the question about the availability of space for privacy was misinterpreted by a few respondents as meaning ownership of land for economic activities. After this, the questionnaire was finalized, formatted, and printed.

Ethical Considerations

As is the case with credible research, and particularly because of the sensitivity associated with human rights issues due to their personal nature, an application for ethical clearance was submitted to the ethics committee of the Department of Commerce and Administration at Walter Sisulu University. After reviewing the application, it was sent to the Walter Sisulu Institutional Ethics Committee for further consideration. The application for ethical clearance for this study was approved by the institutional ethics committee on 26 April 2022, with reference 2022/STAFF/THS/1352.

Data Collection

Data for this study were collected simultaneously from the Northwest, Southwest, and Littoral regions of Cameroon from 15 July to 30 October 2022. Prior to data collection, field workers were selected and trained to ensure adherence to ethical conduct, understanding of the instrument's questions, and familiarity with the research sites or communities. Two lecturers with research expertise from two local universities volunteered to work with the researcher during the training of field workers and the data collection exercise. The field workers were selected based on their prior research experience, ability to communicate in the local language and English, and expert knowledge of the study site or the communities where the IDPs lived.

Training for field workers took place from 5 July to 10 July 2022. Once in the field, the protocol to approach IDPs for data collection was streamlined as follows: the field worker initiated the conversation with the traditional greeting, asked questions aimed at ensuring that the potential respondent was an IDP, explained the purpose of the study, and asked if they would be willing to take part in the study. Those IDPs who gave their consent to participate in the study were either handed the questionnaire to complete or had it read to them, and their responses were noted on the questionnaire.

Data Analysis

The data was analyzed using both descriptive and exploratory statistics. While the descriptive analysis focused on obtaining the general profile and characteristics of the participants, the exploratory analysis aimed to identify any underlying patterns and associations. The data was initially captured on a Microsoft Excel spreadsheet and analyzed using the IBM Statistical Package for Social Sciences (SPSS) version 27.

1.7 Conclusion

This chapter has established the conceptual and contextual foundations for understanding internal displacement. It has been shown that displacement is a complex and multifaceted phenomenon shaped by conflict, environmental change, and structural inequality.

The next chapter builds on this foundation by exploring the historical and religious dimensions of displacement, providing deeper insight into the forces shaping displacement across time and societies.

CHAPTER 2

Historical and Religious Contexts of Internal Displacement

Abstract

This chapter explores the historical and religious dimensions of internal displacement, tracing its evolution from ancient societies to contemporary contexts. It demonstrates that displacement is not a recent phenomenon, but a recurring feature of human history shaped by power, conflict, and structural inequalities.

The chapter also examines the role of religion as both a driver of displacement and a source of resilience and identity. By integrating historical and religious perspectives, the chapter provides a deeper understanding of the forces shaping internal displacement and sets the foundation for analyzing human rights frameworks in subsequent chapters.

Keywords: internal displacement, history, religion, conflict, identity, resilience

2.1 Introduction

Building on the conceptual foundations established in Chapter 1, this chapter situates internal displacement within broader historical and religious contexts. Understanding displacement requires more than contemporary analysis; it demands an appreciation of the historical processes and belief systems that have shaped patterns of forced migration over time.

This chapter argues that displacement is not an isolated or accidental occurrence but a structural and historically embedded phenomenon. It further highlights that religion plays a dual role—both as a factor contributing to displacement and as a resource for coping, identity, and resilience.

2.2 Historical Context of Forced Human Displacement

2.2.1 Displacement in Ancient and Pre-Modern Societies

Forced displacement has been a central feature of human history, often used as a tool of conquest and control. Ancient empires such as the Assyrian and Babylonian states systematically relocated populations to weaken resistance and consolidate power (Deportation practices in ancient empires have been widely documented in historical literature).

Similarly, the Roman Empire employed exile, enslavement, and forced migration as mechanisms of imperial governance. In these contexts, displacement was normalized and rarely questioned, reflecting the absence of formal human rights frameworks.

2.2.2 Medieval and Early Modern Transformations

During the medieval and early modern periods, displacement became increasingly linked to religious and political conflict. The expulsion of Jews and Muslims from Spain in 1492 and the displacement caused by the Thirty Years' War illustrate how identity and belief systems shaped patterns of exclusion and migration (Marrus, 1985).

This period marked a transition from displacement as a tool of conquest to displacement as a mechanism of social and political exclusion, particularly within emerging nation-states.

2.2.3 Colonialism and the Globalization of Displacement

The colonial era significantly expanded the scale and impact of displacement. European expansion led to the forced movement of millions through systems such as the transatlantic slave trade and the dispossession of indigenous populations (Rodney, 1972).

Colonial policies disrupted traditional livelihoods, restructured economies, and entrenched inequalities that continue to influence contemporary displacement patterns in Africa and beyond.

2.2.4 Nation-State Formation and Mass Displacement

The rise of modern nation-states in the nineteenth and early twentieth centuries introduced new forms of displacement linked to nationalism and identity politics. Efforts to create homogeneous populations often resulted in forced migration, ethnic cleansing, and exclusion (Zolberg et al., 1989).

Examples such as the Armenian Genocide and population exchanges in Europe highlight how displacement became intertwined with questions of citizenship and belonging.

2.2.5 World Wars and the Emergence of Protection Frameworks

The two World Wars marked a turning point in the global recognition of displacement. The unprecedented scale of forced migration led to the development of international legal frameworks aimed at protecting displaced populations, including the establishment of the United Nations and the adoption of the 1951 Refugee Convention (UN, 1951).

However, these frameworks primarily focused on refugees, leaving internally displaced persons without equivalent legal protection.

2.2.6 Contemporary Dynamics of Internal Displacement

In the contemporary era, displacement is increasingly complex and multi-causal, driven by conflict, environmental change, and development pressures. A defining feature of modern displacement is its protracted nature, with many individuals remaining displaced for extended periods (IDMC, 2024).

Additionally, displacement is increasingly urban, with many IDPs residing in informal settlements rather than camps, further complicating identification and assistance.

2.3 Religious Contexts of Human Displacement

2.3.1 Religion as a Driver of Displacement

Religion has historically been a significant factor in displacement, often intersecting with political and ethnic tensions. Religious persecution, sectarian violence, and exclusion have forced communities to flee their homes (Ferris, 2011).

In contemporary contexts, religion continues to play a role in shaping conflict dynamics, particularly in regions where religious identity is closely tied to political and social structures.

2.3.2 Sacred Narratives and Meaning-Making

Religious traditions often contain narratives of exile, migration, and survival, which provide frameworks for interpreting displacement experiences. These narratives can transform displacement into a meaningful journey, offering hope and resilience (Levitt, 2007).

2.3.3 Religion, Identity, and Belonging

For displaced populations, religion can serve as a source of identity and belonging, particularly in unfamiliar environments. It provides continuity and social cohesion, helping individuals navigate the challenges of displacement.

However, religious identity can also contribute to exclusion and discrimination in host communities.

2.3.4 Religion as a Source of Resilience

Religious beliefs and practices often play a crucial role in coping with the psychological and emotional impacts of displacement. Faith-based support networks can provide both material and emotional assistance (Ager & Ager, 2011).

2.3.5 Faith-Based Organizations and Humanitarian Response

Faith-based organizations are key actors in humanitarian responses, particularly in Africa. Their local presence and community trust enable them to deliver assistance effectively, although challenges related to neutrality and inclusivity remain (Ferris, 2011).

2.3.6 Religion, Conflict, and Displacement

Religion often interacts with broader socio-political factors, making it difficult to isolate as a single cause of displacement. Instead, it should be understood as part of a complex web of influences shaping conflict and migration.

2.3.7 Religion and Human Rights

From a human rights perspective, religion is both a protected right and a potential source of vulnerability. Ensuring freedom of religion is essential in displacement contexts, where violations are common.

From a human rights perspective, religion is both a source of vulnerability and a basis for protection. The right to freedom of religion or belief is enshrined in international human rights instruments, including the Universal Declaration of Human Rights (United Nations, 1948). However, violations of this right are common in displacement contexts, where religious minorities may face targeted violence or discrimination.

The United Nations Guiding Principles on Internal Displacement emphasize the importance of non-discrimination and the protection of cultural and religious identity (United Nations, 1998). Integrating religious considerations into protection frameworks is therefore essential for ensuring inclusive and effective responses to displacement.

2.4 Conclusion

This chapter has demonstrated that internal displacement is deeply rooted in historical processes and shaped by religious dynamics. Understanding these dimensions provides critical insight into the structural nature of displacement and its persistence across time.

The next chapter builds on this foundation by examining the legal and human rights frameworks that govern the protection and assistance of internally displaced persons.

CHAPTER 3

Human Rights Law and Internal Displacement

Abstract

Building on the conceptual and historical foundations established in the preceding chapters, this chapter examines the legal and institutional frameworks developed to protect and assist internally displaced persons (IDPs). It situates internal displacement within international human rights law and explores key instruments, including the Universal Declaration of Human Rights, the Guiding Principles on Internal Displacement, the African Union's Kampala Convention, and the International Organization for Migration (IOM) framework.

While these frameworks represent significant normative progress, the chapter argues that their effectiveness is undermined by weak implementation. It therefore proposes practical strategies to bridge the gap between policy and practice.

Keywords: human rights law, internal displacement, Kampala Convention, humanitarian law, implementation

3.1 Introduction

Chapter 2 examined the historical and religious foundations of displacement, demonstrating its deep roots in human societies. Building on this foundation, this chapter shifts focus to the legal and institutional mechanisms designed to protect internally displaced persons.

Despite the existence of multiple frameworks, IDPs continue to face severe human rights challenges. This chapter, therefore, explores not only what frameworks exist but also why they often fail in practice.

The discussion is guided by four key questions:

1. What are the origins and foundations of human rights?
2. Why is human rights law central to internal displacement?
3. What frameworks exist to protect IDPs?
4. How can these frameworks be simplified and made accessible?

3.2 Origins and Theoretical Foundations of Human Rights

Human rights theory originates from philosophical traditions emphasizing the inherent dignity of all individuals. Locke (1689/1988) conceptualized rights as natural and inalienable, including life, liberty, and property.

Over time, the concept evolved significantly. The adoption of the Universal Declaration of Human Rights (UDHR) marked a shift toward a comprehensive framework encompassing civil, political, economic, social, and cultural rights (United Nations [UN], 1948).

Subsequent developments expanded human rights to include the fulfilment of basic needs and well-being (UN, 2004). In this context, human rights for internally displaced persons can be understood as fundamental entitlements inherent to all individuals, regardless of displacement status (Myers, 2017).

3.3 Human Rights Law as a Safeguard for Internally Displaced Persons

Internally displaced persons often fall into a protection gap; they are not refugees and may lack adequate national protection. Human rights law, therefore, serves as the primary safeguard.

Its relevance can be understood through four functions:

- Prevention: Prohibits arbitrary displacement.
- Protection: Guarantees access to essential services.
- Security: Safeguards against violence and abuse.
- Recognition: Affirms equal rights and participation.

Human rights law also provides a normative benchmark for assessing state and institutional responses (UN, 1998).

It is important to distinguish between:

- International Human Rights Law (IHRL): Applies at all times.
- International Humanitarian Law (IHL): Applies during armed conflict.
- International Criminal Law (ICL): Addresses serious violations.

3.4 Guiding Principles on Internal Displacement

The Guiding Principles on Internal Displacement (UN, 1998) represent the most widely recognized global framework for IDP protection.

Key contributions include:

- A comprehensive definition of IDPs.
- Affirmation of equality with other citizens.
- Emphasis on prevention of displacement.
- Recognition of state responsibility.
- Identification of durable solutions.

Although non-binding, the principles have become a global standard for policy and practice (Kälin, 2008).

3.5 African Union Convention for the Protection and Assistance of Internally Displaced Persons in Africa (Kampala Convention)

The Kampala Convention (African Union [AU], 2012) represents a landmark regional framework. Unlike the Guiding Principles, it is legally binding in member states.

Key Features:

- Regional focus on African displacement contexts.
- Legal enforceability through domestic legislation.
- Monitoring and reporting mechanisms.
- Emphasis on prevention and state accountability.

Table 3.1 Key differences between the Guiding Principles (UN, 1998) and the Kampala Convention (AU, 2012)

Feature	Guiding Principles (UN, 1998)	Kampala Convention (AU, 2012)
Scope	Global	Regional (Africa)
Legal status	Non-binding	Legally binding
Implementation	Voluntary	Mandatory for signatories
Monitoring	Limited	Structured reporting mechanisms

Note. Adapted from United Nations (1998) and African Union (2012).

3.6 IOM Framework for Addressing Internal Displacement

The International Organization for Migration (IOM, 2017) framework provides an operational approach to addressing internal displacement.

It emphasizes:

- Multi-stakeholder coordination.
- Government leadership and responsibility.
- Flexible, context-specific responses.
- Integration of humanitarian and development approaches.

The International Organization for Migration's Framework for Addressing Internal Displacement (2017) provides guidance on the organization's work in assisting internally displaced persons. This framework is necessitated by the complex and challenging nature of internal displacement. Firstly, even though IDPs require humanitarian assistance from organizations such as the IOM, the primary responsibility for coordinating any assistance resides with sovereign governments. States hold the primary responsibility to protect these populations and ensure their rights. When requested, IOM works with state actors at all levels on their response to and prevention of internal displacement.

Secondly, the scope of the crisis is global, with constantly shifting dynamics. While the root causes of displacement, such as armed conflicts, are becoming more protracted, new conflicts continue to erupt around the world. Thirdly, internal displacement affects IDPs, host communities, and communities of origin in various ways, so a multi-stakeholder approach is needed in managing and resolving the crisis. Further complicating the dynamics is the fact that the causes of internal displacement are diverse, originating from natural and man-made factors.

This framework aims to assist IOM missions to respond effectively in crisis situations affecting and/or driving the movement of IDPs, both directly as well as in partnership with other humanitarian and non-humanitarian actors.

It is important to note that guiding principles aimed at protecting and supporting internally displaced persons fall within the larger context of international human rights frameworks such as International Human Rights Law (IHRL), International Humanitarian Law (IHL), and the Inter-Agency Standing Committee (IASC) Framework on Durable Solutions for IDPs (2010). Therefore, an understanding of these international human rights prescripts is fundamental to their implementation among IDPs.

This framework bridges the gap between policy and implementation.

3.7 International Legal Frameworks

3.7.1 International Human Rights Law (IHRL)

International Human Rights Law (IHRL) is a composite structure of international treaties aimed at promoting and protecting human rights in all corners of international and domestic spaces. All state signatories are obligated to respect, protect, and uphold human rights laws. International Human Rights Law defines State obligations towards their citizens and other individuals within their jurisdiction. These laws, therefore, apply to all human beings, irrespective of where they find themselves. Table 3.2 below presents key treaties and specific human rights domains that they focus on:

Table 3.1 Key Human Rights treaties and their focus areas

Human Rights Treaty	**Specific Area of Concern**
• Universal Declaration of Human Rights (UDHR), United Nations General Assembly on December 10, 1948.	Right to life, equality in dignity and rights, freedom, and security.
• International Covenant on Civil and Political Rights (ICCPR), General Assembly resolution 2200A (XXI), 1966	Right to self-determination, civil and political freedom.
• International Covenant on Economic, Social and Cultural Rights (ICESCR). United Nations General Assembly resolution 2200A (XXI), 1966	Right to housing, food, and health.
• Convention on the Elimination of All Forms of Discrimination Against Women (CEDAW). United Nations General Assembly resolution 34/180, 1979.	Protection of displaced women and girls.

• Convention on the Elimination of All Forms of Racial Discrimination (CERD). UN General Assembly resolution 2106 (XX), 1965.	Protection from racial discrimination.

Note. Compiled from UN (1948, 1966a, 1966b).

Internally Displaced Persons are entitled to the benefits and protection of all human rights treaties, even though they live within the confines of their countries of origin.

3.7.2 International Humanitarian Law (IHL)

IHL applies during armed conflict and includes the Geneva Conventions (1949), which prohibit forced displacement except under specific conditions. The distinction between international humanitarian law and international human rights law is important because while international humanitarian law is applied during armed conflicts to protect civilians from displacement, international human rights law is always enforced to ensure that the basic rights of all human beings are upheld. Two examples of international humanitarian law are the Geneva Conventions (1949) and Additional Protocols, which prohibit forced displacement except when necessary for security or military reasons. Customary international humanitarian law also provides additional protection, especially for vulnerable groups.

The Inter-Agency Standing Committee (IASC) Framework on Durable Solutions for IDPs (2010) focuses on achieving safe and dignified solutions for the crisis of internal displacement.

Emphasis is placed on the voluntary return of internally displaced people to their place of origin. The framework also prioritizes the integration of internally displaced persons into the host community and their resettlement in another part of the country.

3.7.3 Durable Solutions Framework

The Inter-Agency Standing Committee (IASC, 2010) proposes a framework for providing long-term solutions to the precarious situation of internally displaced persons (IDPs). Central to the definition and attainment of durable solutions is the assurance that human rights, humanitarian law, development, reconstruction, and peacebuilding prevail. Stakeholder engagement and collaboration are key in ensuring that national and local authorities, humanitarian and development actors work together to effectively support IDPs and set up a rights-based process so that:

- IDPs are in a position to make an informed and voluntary decision on the durable solution they would like to pursue.
- IDPs participate in the planning and management of the durable solution so that their needs and rights are considered in recovery and development strategies.
- IDPs have safe, unimpeded, and timely access to all actors supporting the achievement of durable solutions, including non-governmental and international humanitarian or development actors.
- IDPs have access to effective mechanisms that monitor the process and the conditions on the ground.
- And situations of displacement resulting from conflict or violence, they are at least indirectly involved in peace processes.

3.8 The Internal Displacement Paradox

Despite extensive frameworks, internal displacement continues to increase (IDMC, 2024; IOM, 2024), fueled by weak political will, fragile institutions, new and protracted conflicts, climate change, and resource scarcity. This paradox highlights a critical gap between policy and implementation.

A common conundrum and reflection point for researchers and policymakers alike has been in the worsening situation of internal displacement despite multiple frameworks and recommendations put forth to curb the crisis. One central question here is, "Why does the number of internally displaced persons continue to increase even as efforts to arrest the situation intensify? It is essential that this paradox be unraveled and clarified before additional proposals are advanced to mitigate the internal displacement debacle. Extant literature attributes the grievous internal displacement situation to a complex range of persistent and merging factors, namely, the absence of political will or policy implementation.

While the pile of frameworks and policies to prevent internal displacement or mitigate its impacts seems to be gathering dust in libraries, many IDPs continue in the agonizing wait for actions that would either clear the way for them to return to their homes and communities or help them resettle elsewhere. The absence of political will on the part of some governments to implement existing frameworks or recommendations is a significant contributing factor to the persistence of internal displacement. This ineptitude on the part of some states can be attributed to three key factors: the non-binding nature of most frameworks, weak state institutions and failed states. Despite the plethora of frameworks on how to alleviate the internal displacement crisis, only the African Union Convention for the Protection and Assistance of Internally Displaced Persons in Africa (2012) is legally binding on signatory governments. This means all other international frameworks on internal displacement are not legally enforceable. Hence, some countries choose to ignore or selectively comply with some of the prescripts. However, even in countries where national frameworks on internal displacement have been developed, implementation has still been found to be half-hearted, at best. A case in point is Nigeria, where the national policy on internally displaced persons was adopted in 2021 (Federal Ministry of Humanitarian Affairs, Disaster Management and Social Development, 2021), but IDPs still live in overcrowded camps with little or no assistance. Similarly, the Democratic Republic of Congo (DRC) whose Humanitarian Response Plan was recently updated in 2025, has witnessed a dramatic deterioration in the IDP situation (United Nations Humanitarian Co-ordinator for the Democratic Republic of Congo, 2025). Further to the foregoing contexts where state institutions have failed to implement well-intended prescripts to assist IDPs, there is the case of failed states or governments whose authority is limited to just a fraction of the country and are unable to implement policy in certain parts of the country. Somalia, South Sudan, and the Central African Republic are typical examples in Sub-Saharan Africa.

Protracted Armed Conflicts and Insecurity

Another contributing factor to the worsening internal displacement situation in sub-Saharan Africa is the prolonged armed conflicts, which create heightened insecurity. While the situation perpetuating some of the internal armed rebellions, such as in Cameroon, remains in a stalemate, other conflicts have further engulfed previous safe areas, such as in the DRC, and conflicts previously settled through power-sharing agreements, such as in Sudan and South Sudan, have re-ignited. The continuous fighting does not offer any hope for IDPs who desperately want to return to their homes or find new places of safety.

Climate Change and Environmental Disasters

The increased frequency and severity of weather-related events such as floods, droughts, wildfires, and hurricanes have also been blamed for the increased number of internally displaced persons. Heavy rainfall caused mudslides that killed many people and displaced large numbers in Ethiopia (mountainous Gofa region in 2024), Uganda (Bulambuli district, 2024), Burundi (Bujumbura, Cibitoke, and Bubanza, 2029), and Sierra Leone (Freetown, 2017). These El Niño-induced floods destroyed homes and displaced thousands of people.

Resource Scarcity

The scarcity of essential resources such as water, food, land, and energy is forcing people to leave their homes and local communities in search of more affluent places. When life-sustaining resources become overused due to population growth, poor management, or environmental degradation, competition for those resources intensifies, prompting conflict and displacement. This is quite characteristic of communal conflicts and internal displacement in Nigeria (Anierobi et al., 2024). Watson (2023) purports that about 90% of communal conflicts in Nigeria originate from land disputes. These conflicts have been explained on competing needs for land, land-based resources, and the ancestral claim to land (Von Uexkull & Pettersson, 2018)

3.9 From Rhetoric to Implementation

Despite the plethora of frameworks and prescripts advocating the respect of human rights among internally displaced persons, recent data from the World Migration Report (IOM, 2024) and the Internal Displacement Monitoring Center (IDMC, 2024) points to a worsening of the crisis. The number of internally displaced persons continues to increase without any reported improvements in their living conditions. There is, therefore, a disjunction between the policy articulations and the effective implementation of those policies to alleviate the internal displacement situation. Based on extant literature (UN, 1998; AU, 2012; IOM, 2017), this chapter proposes two strategic action plans to bridge the gap between policy directives and the successful implementation of human rights law among IDPs: One, the four-pillar action approach, and two, a simplified human rights framework.

The four-pillar action strategy is not a new framework but an approach that recommends new rules of engagement in order to make significant improvements in the living conditions of internally displaced persons.

Table 3.3: Strategic pillars for the protection and support of IDPs

Pillar	**Approach**
Stakeholder Engagement	It is important to recognize IDPs as part of the broader society; hence, extensive stakeholder consultation and involvement is essential in rendering meaningful assistance to affected persons. Internal displacement affects the community of origin, host communities, government departments, and other stakeholders. While recognizing the state's primary responsibility to protect and ensure the rights of IDPs, organizations that assist IDPs consider input from other partners. To this end, providing meaningful assistance and protection to IDPs should work hard to improve transparency, localize funding, increase partnerships, and increase participatory programming.
Respect for International Humanitarian Law (protocols, principles, policies, and practices).	The absence of respect for law and order is anarchy and disorder. Significant progress in improving the conditions of IDPs can only be achieved through the respect of international norms and principles.
Prioritize Human Dignity and Well-Being	Governments and organizations that are committed to ensuring the rights and well-being of IDPs should prioritize their dignity and well-being. This entails conceptualizing assistance from a humanitarian-development nexus through all stages of the displacement cycle. The goal should be to build resilience and self-reliance in the livelihoods of IDPs so that they regain their autonomy as soon as possible.

Inclusive and People-Centered Approach to Service Delivery and Development	Adopting a people-centered and participatory approach ensures that IDPs are not only involved in the decision-making process of issues that concern their welfare but are also happy with the end product. Beyond rendering humanitarian assistance, governments and organizations should incorporate prevention and reduction of displacement strategies as well as longer-term recovery and development strategies into their operations. Responding to internal displacement should be done in collaboration with a range of partners, including states, other international organizations, local and international civil society organizations, development actors, and the private sector. This inclusive approach should focus on disaster and crisis preparedness and planning in relation to natural disasters. This work should emphasize community participation, reduction of vulnerabilities, and strengthening social cohesion.

There is a common practice among government agencies and private sector organizations to engage in assisting internally displaced persons in silos. This fragmented approach to the delivery of aid often leaves some IDPs without the necessary support. Hence, the first pillar in Table 3.1 suggests that there should be stakeholder engagement to undertake a needs analysis of the IDPs prior to the distribution of assistance. It is further recommended that assistance to IDPs be implemented in line with existing humanitarian guidelines and principles to avoid disorderly and uncoordinated activities. Considering the vulnerable situation of IDPs, priority should be given to the dignity and well-being of internally displaced persons. This can be achieved in a number of ways, such as assisting them to become self-reliant, avoiding conditions that push them to be displaced, or taking any related measures. Closely related to ensuring the human dignity and well-being of IDPs is adopting an inclusive approach in decision-making. State parties and other organizations should include IDPs and affected community groups in planning and decision-making processes. This approach should be adopted during all phases (before, during, and after) of displacement.

The second key recommendation from this chapter is a simplified approach to information on human rights prescripts. It is critically important that internally displaced persons know their human rights so that they can report violations.

3.10 Human Rights Prescripts at a Glance

While the Guiding Principles on Internal Displacement (UN, 1998) can be considered the baseline document for understanding and ensuring the respect of human rights among internally displaced persons, other policy frameworks such as the Kampala Convention (AU, 2012) and the Framework for Addressing Internal Displacement (IOM, 2017) equally make an invaluable contribution towards the respect of human rights of IDPs. The challenges involved in protecting the human rights of people forcibly dislodged from their places of permanent residence require the commitment of individuals, organizations, and state agencies to overcome. Considering the traumatic situations characterized by deprivation, injustice, and other forms of hardship that IDPs often endure, individuals, communities, and organizations must be made aware of their human rights. Therefore, it is incumbent on local authorities, international humanitarian agencies, and society in general to ensure that the human rights of IDPs are respected and upheld at all times. A snapshot of the basic rights of IDPs is presented in Figure 3.1 below.

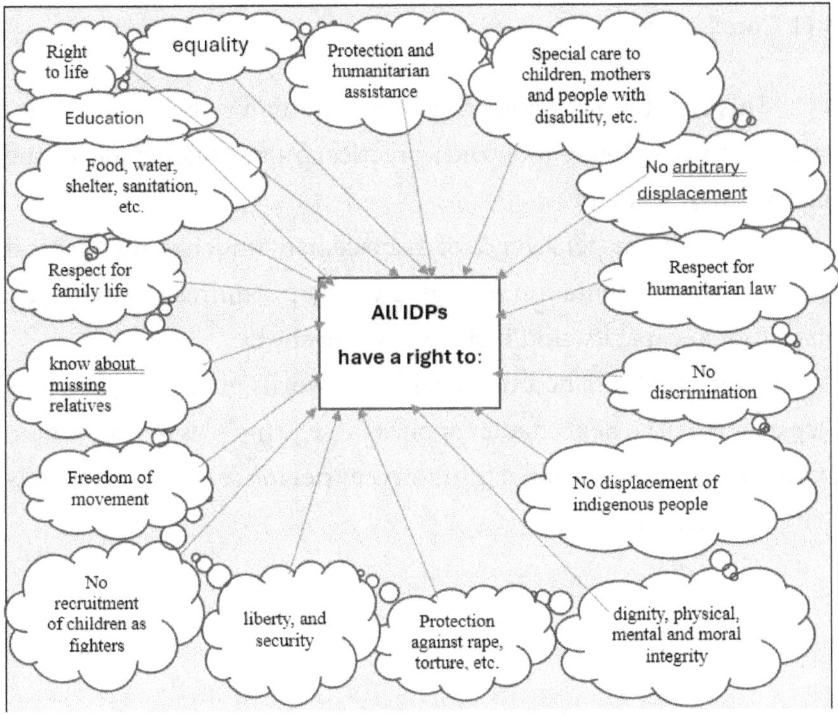

Figure 1. Human Rights framework for internally displaced persons.

Source: Acha-Anyi (2024, Page 285)

An important feature reflected in Figure 3.1 is the interconnectedness of the different human rights prescripts. This explains why each human rights ordinance is connected to all the others. In other words, the ideal is to ensure that the human rights of IDPs are protected on all fronts, recognizing that failure to uphold any one of the human rights regulations amounts to not protecting the human rights of the people concerned (Amnesty International, 2022). The illustrated human rights framework (Figure 2.1) is important in this study, as it serves as a benchmark for assessing IDPs' perceptions of their human rights experiences.

3.11 Conclusion

This chapter has demonstrated that human rights law provides both a normative foundation and a practical framework for addressing internal displacement.

However, the persistence of displacement underscores a critical challenge: implementation. Bridging this gap requires political will, institutional capacity, and inclusive approaches.

Having established the legal frameworks governing internal displacement, the next chapter applies these principles to Cameroon, examining how human rights are experienced in a conflict-driven context.

CHAPTER 4

Cameroon: Conflict and Political Marginalization

Abstract

This chapter examines the experiences of internally displaced persons (IDPs) in Cameroon through an Africa-centered human rights lens. Drawing on quantitative and qualitative data, it analyses how the Anglophone crisis has produced complex patterns of displacement and rights deprivation. The chapter integrates rights-based, capability, human security, and African relational perspectives to demonstrate that internal displacement is a multidimensional human rights crisis shaped by structural inequalities and governance failures. Comparative insights from Nigeria, South Sudan, and the Democratic Republic of Congo (DRC) situate Cameroon within broader continental dynamics. The findings highlight the interdependence of rights and underscore the need for contextually grounded, rights-based interventions that address both immediate vulnerabilities and systemic drivers of displacement.

Keywords: Internal displacement, human rights, Cameroon, Anglophone crisis, Africa, capability approach

4.1 Introduction

This chapter marks the first of three country case studies examining the human rights realities of internally displaced persons (IDPs) across diverse African contexts. Building on the theoretical and methodological foundations established in earlier chapters, it focuses on Cameroon, where internal displacement is primarily driven by armed conflict and political marginalization associated with the Anglophone crisis.

While the preceding chapters conceptualized internal displacement as a multidimensional human rights issue, this chapter provides empirical grounding by illustrating how these dynamics unfold in a conflict setting. It demonstrates how governance deficits, identity-based tensions, and state responses shape patterns of displacement and access to rights.

Importantly, this chapter sets the foundation for comparative analysis by highlighting how conflict-induced displacement disrupts civic freedoms, economic stability, and personal security. The next chapter builds on this by shifting the focus from conflict to environmental and socio-economic displacement in South Africa, thereby expanding the analytical scope of the study.

Internal displacement remains one of the most pressing human rights challenges in Africa, where protracted conflicts, weak governance structures, and socio-economic inequalities converge to produce large-scale population movements (Adeola, 2020; African Union, 2019). In Cameroon, the Anglophone crisis has generated widespread displacement, exposing civilians to multiple and overlapping rights violations.

4.2 Theoretical Framework: African-Centered Human Rights Perspectives

4.2.1 Rights-Based Approach and Legal Pluralism

The rights-based approach (RBA) conceptualizes IDPs as rights-holders and states as duty-bearers obligated to respect, protect, and fulfil human rights (OHCHR, 2006). However, in African contexts, the implementation of rights is often mediated by legal pluralism, where formal legal systems coexist with customary and informal governance structures (Okafor, 2007).

Okafor (2007) argues that African human rights regimes must be understood not only through international legal instruments but also through local socio-political realities. In the context of displacement, this means that access to rights is often negotiated through community networks, traditional authorities, and humanitarian actors rather than solely through formal state institutions.

4.2.2 The Capability Approach and African Communitarianism

The capability approach (Sen, 1999; Nussbaum, 2011) emphasizes individuals' ability to achieve valued ways of living. In African contexts, this framework is enriched by communitarian philosophies such as Ubuntu, which foreground interdependence, dignity, and collective well-being (Metz, 2011).

From this perspective, displacement disrupts not only individual capabilities but also communal structures that sustain livelihoods, identity, and social cohesion. As Ndlovu-Gatsheni (2013) notes, colonial legacies and postcolonial governance failures have produced enduring inequalities that shape contemporary experiences of marginalization, including displacement.

4.2.3 Human Security and Structural Violence

The human security framework (UNDP, 1994) expands the notion of security to include economic, social, and environmental dimensions. In Africa, this perspective intersects with the concept of structural violence, which refers to systemic inequalities that constrain life opportunities (Galtung, 1969; Stewart, 2008).

In contexts such as South Sudan and the DRC, displacement is not only a result of armed conflict but also of chronic governance failures and resource inequalities (Autesserre, 2010). Similarly, in Cameroon, structural marginalization of Anglophone regions has contributed to both conflict and displacement.

4.2.4 Intersectionality and Vulnerability

African feminist scholars highlight the importance of intersectionality in understanding displacement, particularly the ways in which gender, age, and socio-economic status shape vulnerability (Tamale, 2020). Women, children, and the elderly often experience displacement differently, facing heightened risks of exploitation, exclusion, and violence.

4.3 Contextualizing Human Rights Law and Internal Displacement in Cameroon

From a policy perspective, the commitment of the government of Cameroon to the respect for human rights law in general, and among internally displaced persons in particular, is evident in the number of international treaties to which the country is a signatory. Soon after claiming its status as an independent state in the 1960s, the country committed itself to various human rights treaties such as the International Covenant on Civil and Political Rights (UN, 1966), the International Covenant on Economic, Social and Cultural Rights (UN, 1966), and the African Charter for Human and Peoples' Rights (AU, 1981). Recent engagements, such as the United Nations Sustainable Development Cooperation Framework for Cameroon 2022–2026

(UN, 2021), identify "Human rights and dignity for all" as one of the six pillars to guide the realization of the United Nations Sustainable Development Goals in Cameroon. It is worth noting that the United Nations Sustainable Development Cooperation Framework is the main instrument through which the Government of Cameroon and the United Nations system cooperate towards the realization of the national priorities of the Sustainable Development Goals (SDGs) in the country. With specific reference to the respect for human rights among IDPs, the Cameroon government's commitment to the African Union Convention for the Protection and Assistance, commonly referred to as the Kampala Convention, was demonstrated through its ratification in 2015 (Fomekong, 2021). Further to this African Union obligation, Cameroon, as a member of the United Nations General Assembly, is bound by the prescripts of the United Nations' Guiding Principles on Internal Displacement (UN, 1998). Hence, internally displaced persons in the country have multiple human rights frameworks to which they have recourse for protection and support.

4.4 Background and Study Context of the "Anglophone Crisis" in Cameroon

The Anglophone crisis, as the armed insurgency in the two English-speaking regions of Cameroon is commonly called, is deeply rooted in the complex colonial history of the country (ICG, 2022). The initial phase of the colonization of Cameroon began on 14 July 1884, when the German explorer Gustav Nachtigal annexed the Douala coast and established German administration as colonial masters (Ngoh, 2001). Following Germany's defeat in the First World War, however, German Kamerun was ceded to Britain and France, who divided the territory into two parts, with 80% under French administration and 20% under British colonial rule (Konings & Nyamnjoh, 1997).

Whereas in 1960, French-administered Cameroon gained independence as La Republique du Cameroun (the Republic of Cameroon), their counterparts under British rule were asked in a 1961 plebiscite to choose between joining Nigeria or reunifying with La Republique du Cameroun (Ngoh, 2001). Under the auspices of the United Nations, the results of the plebiscite on 11 February 1961 revealed that most British-administered Southern Cameroonians voted to reunite with La Republique du Cameroun (Lazar, 2019).

Despite the terms of the founding agreement stating that the "new" republic would be governed as a federation (Federal Republic of Cameroon) with two centers of power, the first president of the country, Ahmadu Ahidjo, changed the governing structure of Cameroon to a unitary state in 1972, and his successor (Paul Biya) further changed the name of the country back to La Republic du Cameroun in 1984, thereby effectively obliterating the British administrative system that Southern Cameroons brought to the union (Bang & Balgah, 2022). Since the reunification of the two regions, English-speaking Cameroonians (Anglophones), who constitute 14% of the population (World Bank, 2017), have consistently complained of marginalization by their French-speaking counterparts (Konings & Nyamnjoh, 1997).

The spark that started the armed insurgency, however, did not ignite until October 2016, when a peaceful march by the lawyers' and teachers' unions to protest the use of French in the courts and classrooms (Lazar, 2019). In the repression that ensued, leaders of the protests were arrested and locked up. Some of the protesters and their sympathizers ran into the bushes and forests, where they took up arms to fight for an independent state.

Amnesty International (2022) reports that both the separatist fighters and the government forces in Cameroon have committed various human rights violations in the Northwest and Southwest (Anglophone) regions of the country. While women and children have been said to endure most of the suffering from the war, it has also been observed that some women have played prominent roles during the crisis, such as fighting alongside the separatists, leading peace marches, and taking care of their families (ICG, 2022). Mafany and Budi (2019) argue that the crisis in the Anglophone region of Cameroon has significantly aggravated the problem of internal displacement in the country, as it was already grappling with (a) internal displacements caused by Boko Haram attacks in the North, and (b) refugees from the war in the Central African Republic in the Eastern region of the country.

This study focuses on IDPs from the insurgency in the Northwest and Southwest regions of Cameroon, because, unlike other humanitarian situations in the Northern and Eastern regions, this crisis is self-inflicted from within the country, and resolving the contentious issues lies within the influence and authority of local actors. The United Nations Office for the Coordination of Humanitarian Affairs (OCHA) asserts that most IDPs from the Anglophone regions have either fled to safer areas within their region or to the Littoral region, which shares a border with the Southwest region (OCHA, 2021). Data released by Human Rights Watch (2023) reveals that there are 598,000 IDPs as a result of the ongoing fighting in the Anglophone region of Cameroon (HRW, 2023).

4.5 Quantitative Findings: Patterns of Rights Deprivation

4.5.1 Demographic Dynamics and Structural Inequality

Of the 700 questionnaires distributed among the IDP community in the three regions of Cameroon, 529 fully completed and usable responses were received, giving a response rate of 75.6%. The collected data were analyzed using structural equation modelling (SEM) via SmartPLS to assess the direct and indirect effects of biographical factors on the dependent variables. The analysis involved:

- Exploratory and Confirmatory Factor Analysis (EFA & CFA) to validate latent constructs.
- Path analysis to identify direct relationships between biographical factors and human rights dimensions.
- Mediation analysis to assess indirect effects and the role of intervening variables.

Additional statistical tests included descriptive statistics (means, standard deviations, frequencies) and inferential analyses (t-tests, ANOVA, and correlation tests) to determine significant differences across demographic groups.

The descriptive results presented in Table 4.1 below address the first research question by revealing the profiles of the internally displaced persons who participated in this study.

Table 4.1: Demographic characteristics of respondents.

Variable	Description	Frequency	Percentage
Location of IDPs	Northwest region	229	43.3
	Littoral region	200	37.8
	Southwest region	100	18.9
Origin of IDPs	Kumbo	73	13.8
	Fundong	14	2.6
	Njikwa	48	9.1
	Nso	19	3.6
	Santa	122	23.1
	Bafut	77	14.6
	Kumba	176	33.3
Reasons for Displacement	Flooding	5	.9
	War	517	97.7
	Fire	7	1.3
Gender	Male	163	30.8
	Female	366	69.2
Age	18 - 25	182	34.4
	26 – 35	216	40.8
	36 – 45	87	16.4
	46 – 55	28	5.3
	56 – 65	6	1.1
	65+	10	1.9
Employment Status	Unemployed	168	31.8
	Self-employed	259	49.0
	Government employee	53	10.0
	Private sector employee	49	9.2

Education Status	No formal education	25	4.7
	Primary school	241	45.6
	Pre-University	161	30.4
	University	46	8.7
	First degree	15	2.8
	Postgraduate degree	41	7.7

The predominance of women (69.2%) and younger adults between the ages of eighteen and thirty-five years (76.2%) among IDPs reflects broader African displacement trends, where gendered and generational vulnerabilities shape mobility and survival strategies (Adeola, 2020). Limited education and high unemployment further constrain access to economic opportunities, reinforcing cycles of poverty and exclusion.

4.5.2 Civic and Political Rights

The findings in Table 4.2 below reveal the extent to which internally displaced persons (IDPs) feel free to exercise their cultural, religious, linguistic, and political rights without fear. The aim is to assess whether displacement has affected their ability to participate in civic life and express their identities freely.

The analysis focuses on respondents' perceptions of freedom in cultural expression, religious practice, language use, and electoral participation.

Table 4.2 Perceived freedom and cultural expression.

		Never		Hardly		Sometimes		Often		Always		Chi Square p-value
		No.	%	No.	%	No.	%	No.	%	No.	%	
You feel free to practice your culture without fear (B1)	B1	45	8.5	103	19.5	157	29.7	32	6.0	192	36.3	< 0.001
You feel free to practice your religion without fear (B2)	B2	19	3.6	178	33.6	30	5.7	49	9.3	253	47.8	< 0.001
You feel free to speak your language without fear (B3)	B3	11	2.1	70	13.2	181	34.2	36	6.8	231	43.7	< 0.001
You have a right to vote during elections (B4)	B4	98	18.5	142	26.8	117	22.1	62	11.7	110	20.8	< 0.001

While some respondents reported relative freedom in cultural and religious expression, political participation remains significantly constrained. This mirrors findings from Nigeria and South Sudan, where displaced populations are often excluded from formal political processes (IDMC, 2022).

4.5.3 Economic and Social Rights

The results presented in Figure 4.1 below show the ability of internally displaced persons (IDPs) to access essential resources such as food, clean water, healthcare, and education. The analysis identifies disparities in economic security and social well-being among IDPs.

Figure 4.1 Economic and social rights

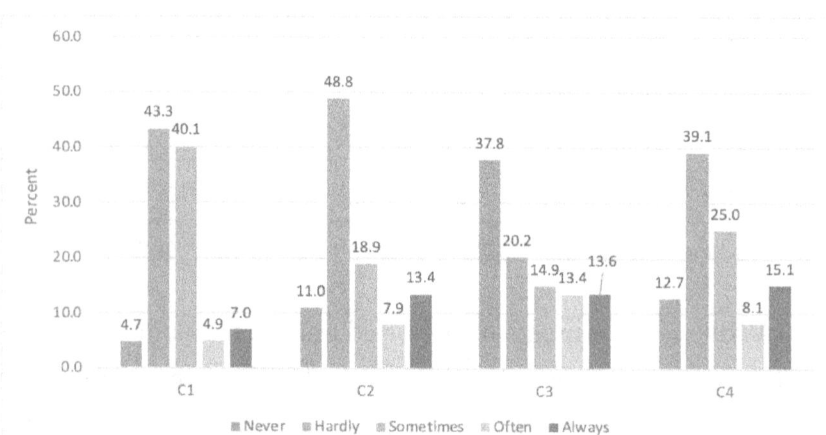

- **Access to Food (C1):** A large proportion of respondents (83.4%) indicated that they do not have enough food to eat daily, indicating widespread food insecurity. Only 7.0% reported always having enough food, while 4.7% stated they never do.
- **Access to Clean Drinking Water (C2):** Nearly half of the respondents (48.8%) indicated that they hardly have access to good drinking water, while 18.9% reported sometimes having access. Only 13.4% reported having clean water, highlighting significant concerns about water availability and quality.
- **Access to Healthcare (C3):** A substantial portion of respondents (37.8%) reported that their right to good health is never protected, while another 20.2% stated that they hardly receive healthcare. A relatively small proportion (13.6%) reported that their healthcare rights are always

protected. This indicates that access to healthcare remains a critical challenge for displaced individuals.

- **Access to Education (C4):** While 39.1% of the participants reported that access to education was difficult for their children or themselves, 25% reported occasional access.

Severe deprivation of food, water, healthcare, and education underscores systemic failures in service delivery. These findings align with studies in the DRC and Somalia, where displacement is closely associated with capability deprivation and humanitarian dependency (Maxwell et al., 2016).

4.5.4 Equality, Protection, and Justice

The study further sought to evaluate the extent to which internally displaced persons (IDPs) feel protected by law enforcement, receive fair treatment in their communities, and experience freedom of movement and expression. The findings in Table 4.3 highlight disparities in security and equal treatment.

Table 4.3 Rights to equality and protection

		Never		Hardly		Sometimes		Often		Always		Chi-Square p-value
		No.	%	No.	%	No.	%	No.	%	No.	%	
Police and security forces worked hard to assist you when you were still in your home (D1)	D1	203	38.4	231	43.7	70	13.2	10	1.9	15	2.8	< .001
Police and security assist you every time you call for help (D2)	D2	230	43.5	237	44.8	29	5.5	14	2.6	19	3.6	< .001
You have been treated equally to everyone in this community (D3)	D3	58	11.0	171	32.3	105	19.8	34	6.4	161	30.4	< .001
You feel free to walk around and talk without fear (D4)	D4	24	4.5	176	33.3	139	26.3	46	8.7	144	27.2	< .001

The perceived absence of state protection reflects a broader crisis of legitimacy and trust in public institutions. Similar patterns have been observed in conflict-affected regions of Nigeria, where security forces are often viewed as ineffective or complicit (Mustapha & Ehrhardt, 2018).

4.5.5 Oppression, Security, and Human Dignity

Further analysis was done to ascertain the extent to which internally displaced persons (IDPs) experience freedom from forced labour, dehumanization, and arbitrary detention. The findings in Table 4.4 highlight varying levels of oppression and mistreatment among IDPs.

Table 4.4 Freedom from oppression

		Never		Hardly		Sometimes		Often		Always		Chi-Square p-value
		No.	%	No.	%	No.	%	No.	%	No.	%	
You have not been treated as a slave (E1)	E1	205	38.8	28	5.3	180	34.0	88	16.6	28	5.3	< .001
People have not treated you as if you are not a human being (E2)	E2	168	31.8	63	11.9	188	35.5	79	14.9	31	5.9	< .001
You have not been arrested and detained without trial (E3)	E3	241	45.6	109	20.6	85	16.1	75	14.2	19	3.6	< .001

Experiences of exploitation, arbitrary detention, and insecurity highlight profound violations of human dignity. These conditions resonate with the concept of structural violence, where systemic inequalities perpetuate harm even in the absence of direct conflict (Galtung, 1969).

4.6 Interconnected Rights: Structural Equation Modelling (SEM) Latent Relationships Using Structural Equation Modelling (SEM)

Structural Equation Modelling (SEM) is used in this study to examine the latent relationships between key human rights dimensions. This approach allows for a comprehensive analysis of how different rights—civic and political freedoms (B), fundamental economic and social rights (C), equality and protection rights (D), freedom from oppression (E), and security and privacy (F)—are interrelated.

By analyzing direct and indirect effects, SEM helps identify the strength and significance of these relationships, revealing how improvements or restrictions in one domain affect others. This analysis is crucial for understanding the systemic nature of human rights experiences among internally displaced persons (IDPs). The findings provide data-driven insights into how social, economic, and security factors interact, informing targeted policy interventions to improve conditions for displaced individuals.

The structural equation model (SEM) fit indices confirm that the model meets all key requirements for reliability and validity. The Chi-square value (569.4693), while significant ($p < 0.001$), is expected given the sample size ($n = 529$). The root mean square error of approximation (RMSEA) is 0.1211, with a low 90% confidence interval (0.1121) and a high 90% confidence interval (0.1304), indicating an acceptable fit. The goodness-of-fit index (GFI = 0.8590) and adjusted goodness-of-fit index (AGFI = 0.7722) demonstrate a strong model fit, while the standardized root mean square residual (SRMR = 0.0741) falls within an acceptable range.

Incremental fit indices also support model adequacy, with the normed fit index (NFI = 0.8635), Tucker-Lewis index (TLI = 0.8270), and comparative fit index (CFI = 0.8764) all approaching the recommended threshold of 0.90, suggesting reasonable model performance.

Construct reliability and validity are well supported. Cronbach's alpha values range from 0.6360 to 0.7923, indicating acceptable internal consistency. The composite reliability (rho_c) values exceed 0.70 for most constructs, confirming reliability. The average variance extracted

(AVE) is above 0.50 for all but one construct (F = 0.4935), indicating strong convergent validity.

Overall, the SEM model demonstrates good construct validity and reliability, providing a robust foundation for analyzing latent relationships between human rights dimensions among internally displaced persons (IDPs).

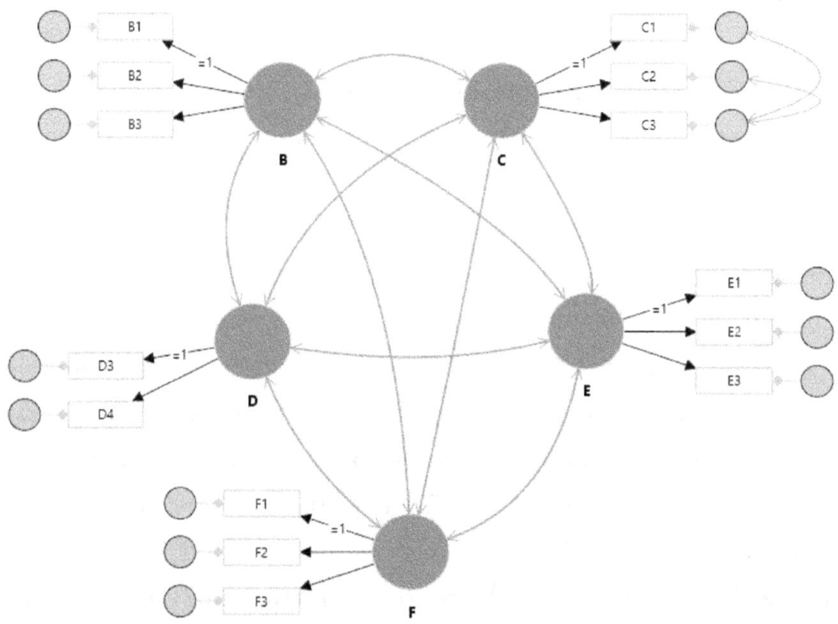

Figure 4.2 The Structural Equation Model (SEM) of the relationship between the variables

The direct effects (without mediation) illustrate the fundamental associations between the different sections, revealing the following relationships:

- Civic and political freedoms (B) and fundamental economic and social rights (C) (*$\beta = 0.250, p < 0.001$*)

- Civic and political freedoms (B) and equality and protection rights (D) ($\beta = 0.842, p < 0.001$)
- Fundamental economic and social rights (C) and equality and protection rights (D) ($\beta = 0.390, p < 0.001$)
- Civic and political freedoms (B) and freedom from oppression (E) ($\beta = -0.562, p < 0.001$)
- Fundamental economic and social rights (C) and freedom from oppression (E) ($\beta = -0.239, p < 0.001$)

Key findings from the SEM:

The SEM analysis confirms the indivisibility and interdependence of human rights, demonstrating that:

- Civic freedoms underpin economic and social rights.
- Economic stability enhances equality and protection.
- Oppression and insecurity are mutually reinforcing.

Biographical factors such as gender, education, and employment significantly mediate these relationships, underscoring the importance of intersectional analysis.

4.7 Qualitative Insights: Lived Realities of Displacement in the Cameroon Context

Of the thirty-five IDPs targeted for the interviews, twenty-eight signed informed consent forms and participated, while seven declined due to personal commitments. This resulted in an 80% response rate for the interviews. The distribution of the interviewees across the three selected regions of Cameroon is summarized in Table 4.5 below:

Table 4.5 Distribution of interview participants among IDPs in Cameroon

Community Group	Study Site (region) and Number of Participants			Total
	A (Northwest)	Southwest	Littoral	
Family head	3	3	4	10
Medical practitioner	2	1	2	5
Security personnel	2	2	2	6
General administration	2	2	3	7
Total	**9 (32%)**	**8 (29%)**	**11 (39%)**	**28**

Since internally displaced persons generally live in makeshift communities, there are few established administrative authorities dedicated to their welfare and protection.

The qualitative findings provide depth and context to the statistical patterns.

Results of the Analysis from the Interviews:

Transcripts of the interviews and notes on points emphasized during the discussions were analyzed using NVivo 15 Qualitative Data Analysis (QDA) software. The analysis focused on generating content and themes that highlight issues of concern to the community, as perceived by the respondents. A cluster analysis of the data is presented in Figure 4.3 below.

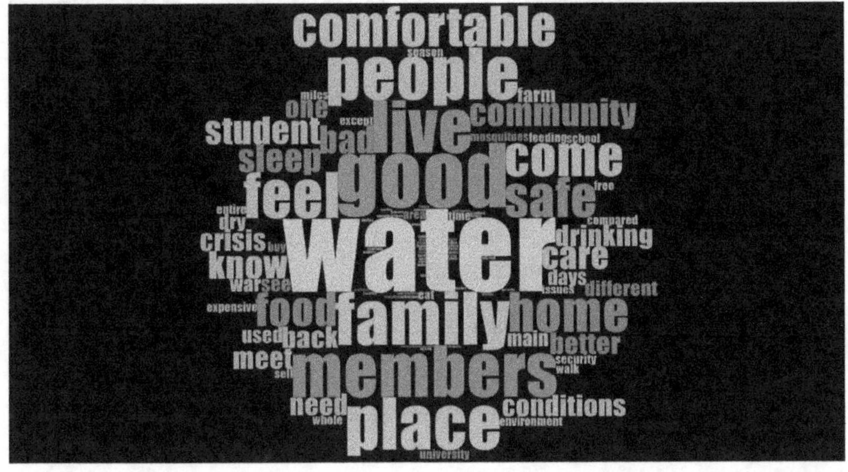

Figure 4.3 Word cloud analysis highlighting the most urgent human rights needs among IDP respondents.

Cause of Displacement—War

The dominant theme from the interviews was the reason why the respondents were forced to flee from their homes and communities. All the respondents emphasized that the heightened insecurity created by the fighting between the state security forces and dissidents fighting for an independent country called Ambazonia was the primary cause of their displacement. Some interviewees explained how they resisted abandoning their homes and livelihoods until some members of their community were killed in the crossfire between the warring parties. In the words of respondent **PP13 (male, aged 47),** "It was the intensification of the Anglophone crisis with the [gunshot] exchanges between the military and the amba fighters in my community." However, one family head **(PP8, female, 51)** pointed out that her "house was put on flames due to the crisis, so I had to leave immediately". A more youthful respondent **(PP21, Male, 29)** who assisted with documenting newly arrived internally displaced persons, bluntly stated that "Actually, the main reason I'm here is for my studies, mainly, so in my area schools are closed."

Impact of Internal Displacement

Families and Communities

The theme of the devastating impact that the war and internal displacement have had on families also featured prominently in the analysis of the interviews. Many respondents spoke passionately about their family members, some of whom had been killed as they tried to flee the fighting, but some of them lamented how they could not account for the whereabouts of their loved ones. One respondent (PP5, male aged forty-eight) exclaimed, "Yes, eight, I have eight of my family members. I don't know [where] to find any of them." Closely related to the impact that the fighting has had on families was that of community life. It was apparent from the interviews that there were deep-rooted community bonds that melted away as the flames consumed their houses.

Livelihoods

Almost all interviewees reported having lost their sources of livelihood. People who were employed explained that they could not go to work because they feared getting killed on their way to work. However, most of the respondents were self-employed on their farms or selling in shops that they owned. All those opportunities had now evaporated, and the IDPs were desperately in need of gainful employment. One respondent (PP1, female aged thirty-four) said, "I used to sell crops to [in] the market, and I was taking care of three of my siblings because I'm the oldest." Asked how they are surviving in the new place of settlement, she replied, "One of my sisters works as a house-help in town and thanks to that, we got money to start up this potatoes business."

Living Conditions—Lack of Essential Services

The absence of basic services and poor living conditions also emerged from the interviews as an issue of concern. Accommodation was reported to be of poor quality as some of the houses had holes through which people in the street could infringe on the privacy of occupants. Decent accommodation was described as expensive and inaccessible to most internally displaced people. In the words of one male respondent (PP11, aged forty-two, living with his wife and two children), "Our living condition is not [too] favorable because we live in a house that is almost falling apart." Another respondent with health challenges complained about the challenges in getting medication. A female respondent (PP15, aged thirty-six) pointed out that "After it rains, you find water to be so muddy." Food was also reported to be in short supply and quite expensive.

Insecurity

The sub-theme of insecurity received mixed reviews from the respondents. While some people reported that their personal items occasionally went missing, others indicated that they felt safer in the new environment. One male respondent (PP19, aged thirty-nine) took a deep breath before explaining that, "It is safer here since we don't have gunshots like we do back at home." And added that "I sleep well."

However, a number of respondents were generally apprehensive of the unknown faces in the new environment.

Highlights from the interviews conducted with IDPs in Cameroon:

Conflict and Forced Migration

Participants consistently identified armed conflict as the primary driver of displacement, often triggered by direct exposure to violence.

Social Disintegration

Displacement disrupts family structures and community cohesion, eroding traditional support systems central to African social organization.

Economic Collapse

Loss of livelihoods is widespread, with respondents describing transitions from self-sufficiency to precarious survival.

Living Conditions and Service Gaps

Poor housing, inadequate sanitation, and limited healthcare access reflect systemic neglect and resource constraints.

Ambivalent Security

While some respondents perceive relative safety away from conflict zones, others remain vulnerable to crime and uncertainty.

4.9 Conclusion and Policy Implications

This chapter demonstrates that internal displacement in Cameroon is a systemic human rights crisis shaped by structural inequalities, governance failures, and conflict dynamics.

A rights-based and Africa-centered approach to policy should prioritize:

- Strengthening institutional accountability and protection mechanisms.
- Addressing structural inequalities, particularly gender and economic disparities.
- Expanding access to essential services and livelihood opportunities.
- Supporting community-based and culturally grounded interventions.

CHAPTER 5

South Africa: Climate, Inequality, and Urban Vulnerability

Abstract

This chapter examines the experiences of internally displaced persons (IDPs) in South Africa, focusing on displacement caused by environmental disasters—particularly flooding—as well as social and economic factors. Using a mixed-methods approach, the chapter integrates quantitative survey data and qualitative interviews to analyze the extent to which civic freedoms, socio-economic rights, equality, and personal security are realized during displacement. Anchored in a rights-based and Africa-centered theoretical framework, the findings reveal that internal displacement in South Africa constitutes a multidimensional human rights crisis shaped by climate vulnerability, structural inequality, and governance deficits. Comparative insights from other African contexts highlight both shared and unique dynamics. The chapter concludes by advocating for integrated, rights-based, and climate-responsive policy interventions.

Keywords: Internal displacement, human rights, climate change, South Africa, socio-economic rights, governance

5.1 Introduction

Following the examination of conflict-driven displacement in Cameroon, this chapter turns to South Africa, where internal displacement is shaped primarily by environmental disasters, socio-economic inequality, and urban vulnerability.

This shift in focus is deliberate. While Cameroon illustrates how political conflict generates displacement, South Africa demonstrates that displacement can also emerge in relatively stable political contexts, driven by climate change and structural inequality. This broadens the analytical lens of the book by introducing climate-induced and socio-economic displacement as critical dimensions of the human rights discourse.

The chapter builds on the findings from Cameroon by showing that, despite differences in drivers, similar human rights challenges persist, including limited access to basic services, insecurity, and inequality. These parallels reinforce the argument that internal displacement is fundamentally a structural issue.

The next chapter extends this comparative trajectory by examining Nigeria, where displacement is driven by a complex interaction of violence, organized crime, and ethno-religious tensions, thereby introducing a third typology of displacement.

Internal displacement in South Africa reflects the intersection of environmental vulnerability, socio-economic inequality, and governance challenges. Internally displaced persons (IDPs), unlike refugees, remain within national borders and depend primarily on domestic institutions for protection and support (Internal Displacement Monitoring Center [IDMC], 2023). This reliance often exposes gaps in state capacity and accountability, resulting in uneven access to rights and services.

In recent years, environmental factors—particularly climate-induced disasters—have emerged as major drivers of displacement. The 2022 KwaZulu-Natal floods, which displaced thousands and caused widespread destruction, illustrate the increasing intensity of climate-related risks (South African Weather Service [SAWS], 2022). These risks disproportionately affect marginalized populations living in informal settlements characterized by inadequate infrastructure and high exposure to environmental hazards (Holloway, 2017).

However, environmental factors alone do not fully explain displacement in South Africa. Historical inequalities rooted in apartheid-era spatial planning continue to shape access to land, housing, and services (Republic of South Africa, 1996). These structural inequalities, combined with high levels of crime and governance shortcomings, create conditions in which displacement is both a symptom and a driver of human rights deprivation.

This chapter examines these dynamics through a mixed-methods approach, combining quantitative survey data with qualitative insights to provide a comprehensive understanding of IDPs' human rights experiences in South Africa.

5.2 Theoretical Framework: Climate, Rights, and Structural Inequality

5.2.1 Rights-Based Approach and State Responsibility

The rights-based approach (RBA) frames displacement as a matter of legal entitlement rather than humanitarian charity, positioning IDPs as rights-holders and the state as the primary duty-bearer (OHCHR, 2006). In South Africa, this framework is reinforced by a progressive constitutional order that guarantees rights to housing, healthcare, education, and security (Republic of South Africa, 1996).

However, as observed across many African contexts, the gap between constitutional guarantees and lived realities reflects limitations in governance capacity and policy implementation (Adeola,

2020). For IDPs, this gap is particularly pronounced during crises, when institutional responses are often delayed or inadequate.

5.2.2 Climate Justice and Environmental Displacement

The concept of climate justice is central to understanding displacement in South Africa. Climate justice emphasizes that environmental harms disproportionately affect vulnerable populations who have contributed the least to climate change (Schlosberg, 2012). In informal settlements, residents face heightened flood risk due to poor urban planning, inadequate drainage systems, and fragile housing structures.

This aligns with broader African experiences, where environmental displacement is increasingly linked to structural inequalities and weak disaster preparedness systems (African Union, 2019).

5.2.3 Capability Approach and Human Security

The capability approach (Sen, 1999) highlights how displacement restricts individuals' ability to achieve well-being by limiting access to essential resources and opportunities. In South Africa, displacement disrupts livelihoods, education, and social networks, thereby constraining both economic and social capabilities.

The human security framework (UNDP, 1994) further broadens this analysis by emphasizing multidimensional insecurity, including economic instability, physical danger, and social exclusion. These dimensions are evident in the lived experiences of IDPs, who face overlapping risks in resettlement environments.

5.2.4 Structural Inequality and Intersectionality

Displacement in South Africa must also be understood through the lens of structural inequality and intersectionality. Marginalized groups—particularly women, children, and the poor—are disproportionately affected by both displacement and its consequences (Tamale, 2020). These inequalities are rooted in historical patterns of exclusion and are reproduced through contemporary governance failures.

5.3 Drivers of Displacement in South Africa

5.3.1 Environmental Drivers

Flooding emerged as the dominant cause of displacement, affecting over 80% of respondents. The 2022 KwaZulu-Natal floods exemplify the growing impact of climate change on vulnerable communities. Informal settlements, often located in flood-prone areas, are particularly at risk due to inadequate infrastructure and limited disaster preparedness.

Other environmental factors, including fires and droughts, also contribute to displacement, although to a lesser extent. Fires, often linked to overcrowding and unsafe energy sources, highlight the intersection of environmental and socio-economic vulnerabilities.

5.3.2 Social and Security Drivers

Crime and violence play a dual role as both triggers and consequences of displacement. High levels of robbery, theft, and gender-based violence create unsafe living conditions, forcing individuals to relocate. In resettlement areas, these risks often persist, undermining recovery efforts and reinforcing cycles of vulnerability.

5.3.3 Economic Drivers

Economic instability, unemployment, and lack of affordable housing contribute to displacement by pushing individuals into precarious living conditions. Migration to urban centers in search of opportunities often results in settlement in informal areas, increasing exposure to environmental risks.

5.3.4 Governance Failures

Governance and service delivery gaps are central to the displacement crisis. Delays in the provision of Reconstruction and Development Programme (RDP) housing, inadequate disaster response, and weak coordination among government agencies exacerbate both displacement and its impacts.

5.4 Quantitative Findings: Human Rights Dimensions

5.4.1 Reliability and Factor Structure

The analysis of survey data indicates moderate to strong reliability across most human rights dimensions, with civic and political freedoms showing the highest internal consistency. Results of the factor analysis (Table 5.1) confirm the multidimensional nature of rights, identifying five key themes:

- Civic and political freedoms.
- Economic and social rights.
- Equality and protection.
- Freedom from oppression.
- Security and privacy.

Table 5.1: Rotated component matrix

	Component				
	1	2	3	4	5
You feel free to practice your culture without fear. (B1)	0.766	0.090	-0.001	0.054	0.137
You feel free to practice your religion without fear. (B2)	0.735	-0.103	0.048	-0.047	0.266
You feel free to speak your language without fear. (B3)	0.670	0.176	0.275	-0.058	-0.169
You have a right to vote during elections. (B4)	0.665	0.155	0.177	-0.020	-0.118
You have enough food to eat every day. (C1)	0.007	0.715	-0.001	0.041	0.079
You have access to good drinking water. (C2)	0.077	0.678	-0.057	0.028	0.267
Your rights to good health are protected here. (C3)	0.209	0.496	0.183	-0.159	0.072
You or your children have the opportunity to go to school. (C4)	0.440	0.457	0.241	-0.095	0.028
Police and security forces worked hard to assist you when you were still in your home. (D1)	0.119	0.039	0.722	0.220	0.021
Police and security assist you every time you call for help. (D2)	0.105	0.083	0.717	0.134	0.082

You have been treated equally by everyone in this community. (D3)	0.207	0.033	0.612	-0.237	0.272
You feel free to walk around and talk without fear. (D4)	0.204	0.246	0.402	-0.153	0.367
You have not been treated as a slave. (E1)	-0.015	-0.013	-0.004	0.774	-0.046
People have not treated you as if you are not a human being. (E2)	-0.047	0.002	0.243	0.747	-0.021
You have not been arrested and detained without trial. (E3)	0.010	-0.391	-0.207	0.513	0.360
You have space to do your private and personal things without people watching you. (F1)	-0.013	0.078	0.059	0.036	0.750
You live in a safe and comfortable house where you do not fear. (F2)	0.061	0.401	0.203	-0.131	0.451
You feel that your life is not in danger in this community. (F3)	0.037	0.256	0.158	0.042	0.422
Extraction Method: Principal Component Analysis. Rotation Method: Varimax with Kaiser Normalization.					
a. Rotation converged in 6 iterations.					

These findings align with the principle of the indivisibility of human rights, emphasizing that rights are interconnected and mutually reinforcing.

Demographic Characteristics of Respondents

The study achieved a high response rate, with 559 questionnaires completed out of 700 distributed, representing a 79.8% response rate. The majority of respondents (72.5%) were located in Durban, while 27.5% were based in Cape Town. The age distribution showed that the largest proportion of respondents (28.3%) were aged between thirty-six and forty-eight years, followed by those aged twenty-six to thirty-five years (24.0%). Males comprised 53.5% of the sample, females 43.8%, and 2.7% identified as "Other." Educational attainment varied, with 23.1% holding a National Diploma, 21.5% having education below university entrance, and only 4.5% possessing postgraduate qualifications. Occupation-wise, unemployment was prevalent, affecting 36.0% of respondents. The remainder were engaged in various forms of employment, including farming, teaching, and domestic work, highlighting the diversity of livelihoods among IDPs.

Causes of Displacement

The study identified multiple causes of internal displacement in South Africa, highlighting the complex interplay of environmental, social, and economic factors. These causes underscore the vulnerabilities faced by marginalized populations and the systemic gaps in addressing displacement effectively.

Environmental Factors

Environmental disasters, particularly flooding, emerged as the primary driver of internal displacement. The study revealed that 82.1% of respondents attributed their displacement to floods, with many referencing the catastrophic 2022 KwaZulu-Natal floods. This disaster destroyed homes, displaced thousands, and disrupted entire communities. Respondents described how rising water levels engulfed their homes and belongings, leaving them with no choice but to flee to temporary shelters or seek refuge with family members in other areas.

The growing intensity and frequency of flooding events are closely linked to climate change, which has intensified extreme weather. Vulnerable populations, particularly those residing in informal settlements, are disproportionately affected. These settlements are often located in low-lying, flood-prone areas and lack the infrastructure needed to withstand such events. Poor drainage systems, inadequate housing structures, and limited disaster preparedness further exacerbate the impact of flooding, leaving residents with few resources to recover.

The study also highlighted how other environmental factors, such as fires and droughts, contribute to displacement, although to a lesser extent. Fires, often caused by unsafe energy sources or overcrowding in informal settlements, accounted for 9.8% of displacement cases. These incidents destroy homes and personal belongings, forcing affected individuals into temporary shelters. While drought was not a major cause among respondents, its broader impacts on rural livelihoods, particularly for those dependent on agriculture, were noted as an indirect driver of displacement in some areas.

Social Factors

Social factors, including crime and violence, were identified as significant contributors to displacement, accounting for 8.1% of reported cases. Respondents described how high crime rates in their communities, particularly robbery, theft, and physical violence, created unsafe living conditions that ultimately forced them to leave their homes. Gender-based violence was a recurring concern, disproportionately affecting women and children. Many women reported fleeing their homes due to domestic violence or threats of sexual violence, highlighting the intersection of displacement and gender inequality.

Additionally, communal tensions and localized conflicts were mentioned as contributing factors. In some cases, disputes over resources, land, or ethnic differences escalated into violence, displacing families from their homes. These findings align with broader trends in South Africa, where social instability and weak law enforcement often exacerbate the vulnerabilities of marginalized communities.

Economic Factors

Economic instability and poverty were cited as indirect drivers of displacement. Respondents described how limited access to affordable housing, combined with rising unemployment and economic hardships, forced them to move to informal settlements or other precarious living arrangements. These areas are often located in environmentally risky zones, making residents more vulnerable to displacement during disasters.

Furthermore, the lack of economic opportunities in rural areas pushes many individuals to urban centers in search of better livelihoods. However, the high cost of living in cities often leaves them in overcrowded, informal housing, further exposing them to displacement risks. This cycle of economic vulnerability and displacement underscores the systemic nature of poverty and its role in exacerbating internal displacement.

Governance and Service Delivery Failures

The study also identified governance and service delivery failures as underlying causes of displacement. Respondents frequently cited delays in the provision of the Reconstruction and Development Programme (RDP) housing and insufficient municipal support as critical challenges. Many displaced individuals reported waiting years for promised housing, only to be placed in overcrowded temporary shelters that lacked basic services such as water, sanitation, and electricity.

Inadequate disaster preparedness and response mechanisms further compounded the issue. Respondents described how local authorities often failed to provide timely warnings or evacuation plans during disasters, leaving residents to fend for themselves. The lack of coordination among government agencies and the absence of long-term recovery plans were also noted as significant contributors to displacement and its prolonged impacts.

Cumulative Impact of Multiple Factors

While individual factors such as flooding, crime, or housing insecurity were significant, the study highlighted how these causes often overlap and compound one another. For example, respondents displaced by floods described how the loss of their homes also led to job loss, increased financial strain, and heightened vulnerability to crime in resettlement areas. Similarly, individuals fleeing violence often found themselves in overcrowded shelters that were prone to fires or lacked basic resources, creating a cycle of displacement and vulnerability.

The findings emphasize that internal displacement in South Africa is not driven by a single factor but rather by a combination of environmental, social, economic, and governance-related challenges. These interrelated causes highlight the need for holistic and integrated approaches to addressing displacement and supporting affected populations.

5.3 Perceptions on the Impacts on Rights

5.3.1 Human Rights and Civic Freedoms

Respondents generally reported varying levels of civic and political freedoms in their new communities. Table 5.3 presents respondents' perceptions regarding the respect of their civic and basic human rights.

Table 5.2: Perceptions on Civic Rights and Political Freedoms

		Never		Hardly		Sometimes		Often		Always		Chi-Square p-value
		No.	%	No.	%	No.	%	No.	%	No.	%	
You feel free to practice your culture without fear (B1)	B1	36	6.5	40	7.2	106	19.0	112	20.1	264	47.3	< 0.001
You feel free to practice your religion without fear (B2)	B2	24	4.3	63	11.3	108	19.3	113	20.2	251	44.9	< 0.001
You feel free to speak your language without fear (B3)	B3	28	5.0	37	6.6	70	12.5	76	13.6	348	62.3	< 0.001
You have a right to vote during elections (B4)	B4	54	9.7	23	4.1	44	7.9	78	14.0	360	64.4	< 0.001

A significant proportion felt free to practice their culture (47.3%), religion (44.9%), and language (62.3%). However, some respondents (6.5%) indicated that they never felt free to express their culture, and 4.3% felt restricted in practicing their religion. The right to vote was widely acknowledged, with 64.4% reporting they always felt this freedom, suggesting that civic participation remains relatively intact, despite displacement. However, feelings of equality and protection were less consistent. Only 24.9% of respondents felt they were always treated equally in their communities, while 30.4% reported experiencing equality "sometimes." Access to police assistance was a significant concern, with only 12.9% stating they always received help when needed.

5.3.2 Socio-Economic Rights

Access to basic needs, such as food and water, was uneven among respondents. Figure 5.2 Perceptions on socio-economic rights.

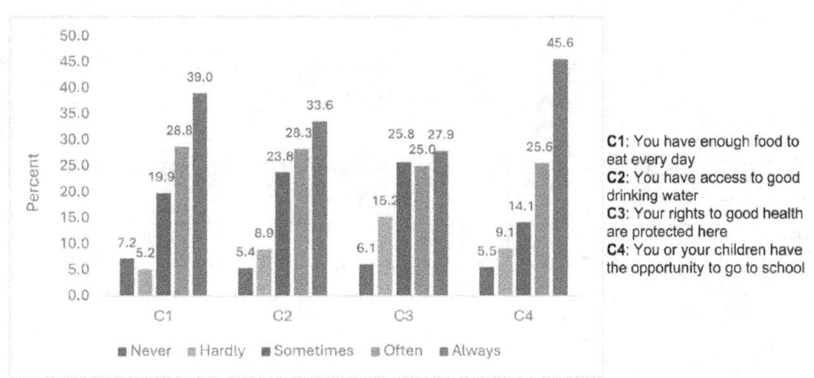

As illustrated in Figure 5.2, 39% of respondents reported unhindered access to food, while 7.2% reported never having enough food. Access to good drinking water was similarly inconsistent: 33.6% reported regular access, while 5.4% reported no access at all. Educational opportunities were somewhat more positive, with 45.6% stating they or their children always had access to schooling. However, a combined 14.6% reported having no or hardly any access to education. Health rights protection emerged as a critical concern, with 15.2% reporting that their health rights were "hardly ever" protected.

5.3.3 Security and Privacy

Perceptions of safety and privacy varied widely among respondents, as shown in Table 4. Only 22.0% felt consistently safe in their homes, while 18.9% reported never or hardly feeling safe. Crime was a pervasive concern in resettlement areas, with respondents frequently citing incidents of robbery, theft, and gender-based violence. Privacy was also limited for many; while 34.9% reported always having personal privacy, 23.5% described limited or no privacy, often due to overcrowded living conditions.

Table 5.3: Perceptions regarding Security and Privacy

		Never		Hardly		Sometimes		Often		Always		Chi-Square p-value
		No.	%	No.	%	No.	%	No.	%	No.	%	
You have space to do your private and personal things without people watching you (F1)	F1	54	9.7	77	13.8	116	20.8	117	20.9	195	34.9	< 0.001
You live in a safe and comfortable house where you do not fear (F2)	F2	32	5.7	74	13.2	160	28.6	170	30.4	123	22.0	< 0.001
You feel that your life is not in danger in this community (F3)	F3	64	11.5	81	14.5	234	41.9	101	18.1	78	14.0	< 0.001

These results indicate that while a considerable number of individuals feel secure in their private lives and homes, there remains a significant segment of the population experiencing a lack of privacy and safety, which is crucial for well-being. This data is instrumental in understanding the degree to which individuals feel their personal rights to privacy and security are being upheld within the community.

5.3.4 Equality and Protection Rights

Respondents expressed mixed perceptions regarding their experiences of equality in their communities. Only 24.9% of respondents felt they were "always" treated equally in their new environments, suggesting that a significant majority either experienced inequality or were uncertain about their treatment. An additional 30.4% indicated that they experienced equality "sometimes," reflecting inconsistent or situational treatment. Meanwhile, 12.7% reported that they "rarely" or "never" felt treated equally, highlighting cases of systemic exclusion and discrimination.

Table 5.4: Perceptions on equality and protection rights

		Never		Hardly		Sometimes		Often		Always		Chi-Square p-value
		No.	%	No.	%	No.	%	No.	%	No.	%	
Police and security forces worked hard to assist you when you were still in your home (D1)	D1	65	11.6	126	22.5	184	32.9	108	19.3	76	13.6	< 0.001
Police and security assist you every time you call for help (D2)	D2	46	8.2	141	25.2	179	32.0	121	21.6	72	12.9	< 0.001
You have been treated equally to everyone in this community (D3)	D3	35	6.3	65	11.6	170	30.4	150	26.8	139	24.9	< 0.001
You feel free to walk around and talk without fear (D4)	D4	24	4.3	46	8.2	199	35.6	149	26.7	141	25.2	< 0.001

The qualitative data provided deeper insights into these disparities. Many respondents felt that their displacement status marked them as "outsiders" in their resettlement areas, leading to unequal access to resources and opportunities. Instances of favoritism in housing allocation and relief distribution were frequently cited, with some respondents alleging that local officials prioritized certain groups over others based on political affiliation, ethnicity, or personal relationships.

The findings also revealed critical gaps in access to protection from law enforcement agencies. Only 12.9% of respondents stated that the police "always" assisted them when called upon, reflecting limited effectiveness in providing security for displaced populations. By contrast, 21.5% indicated that they "never" received police assistance, and 28.3% reported that police intervention occurred "rarely" or "sometimes."

Respondents described how law enforcement often failed to respond to reports of crime in resettlement areas, leaving residents feeling vulnerable and unprotected. Women and children, in particular, highlighted the lack of protection against gender-based violence and harassment, which were pervasive in overcrowded shelters and informal settlements. Many participants expressed frustration with the perceived indifference of law enforcement officials, who they felt prioritized wealthier or more politically connected communities.

Several systemic challenges were identified as barriers to achieving equality and protection for IDPs:

- **Structural Inequality:** Many displaced individuals came from marginalized backgrounds and faced pre-existing inequalities, which were further exacerbated by their displacement.
- **Resource Allocation:** The scarcity of resources in resettlement areas often led to competition and conflict among residents, undermining efforts to promote equality.
- **Governance Gaps:** Delays in the delivery of promised housing and services contributed to perceptions of unequal treatment, as some groups appeared to benefit more quickly than others.
- **Social Stigmatization:** IDPs frequently experienced stigma and discrimination from host communities, which viewed them as burdens or outsiders.

Despite these challenges, there were some positive perceptions regarding protection rights. Respondents who lived in areas with active community policing initiatives or engaged local leaders reported feeling more secure and supported. Collaborative efforts between local governments, non-governmental organizations (NGOs), and community groups were seen as effective in addressing some of the gaps in equality and protection.

5.3.5 Freedom from Oppression

Table 6 presents the respondents' perceptions of their experiences of freedom from oppression, focusing on three key aspects: freedom from slavery (E1), being treated with humanity (E2), and protection from arbitrary arrest and detention without trial (E3). The responses are categorized on a Likert scale ranging from "Never" to "Always," with chi-square p-values provided to assess the statistical significance of the distribution.

Table 5.5: Freedom from oppression

		Never		Hardly		Sometimes		Often		Always		Chi-Square p-value
		No.	%	No.	%	No.	%	No.	%	No.	%	
You have not been treated as a slave (E1)	E1	245	43.8	67	12.0	102	18.2	54	9.7	91	16.3	< 0.001
People have not treated you as if you are not a human being (E2)	E2	154	27.5	57	10.2	171	30.6	87	15.6	90	16.1	< 0.001
You have not been arrested and detained without trial (E3)	E3	360	64.4	27	4.8	37	6.6	32	5.7	103	18.4	< 0.001

A significant proportion of respondents (43.8%) indicated that they "never" felt free from being treated as a slave, while 16.3% reported "always" feeling free from such treatment. Additionally, 18.2% responded "sometimes," and smaller percentages chose "hardly" (12.0%) and "often" (9.7%). The chi-square p-value (<0.001) indicates that the distribution of responses is statistically significant, suggesting variation in perceptions among respondents.

These findings suggest that while a notable proportion of respondents feel free from being treated as a slave, a substantial percentage (approximately 56.2%) expressed varying degrees of uncertainty or negative experiences. This highlights potential instances of economic or social exploitation, where displaced individuals may feel coerced into labor or treated unjustly due to their vulnerable status.

About 27.5% of respondents reported that they "never" felt they were treated as a human being, while 16.1% stated they "always" felt this way. The largest group (30.6%) responded "sometimes," and the remaining respondents reported "hardly" (10.2%) or "often" (15.6%). The chi-square p-value (<0.001) confirms significant variation in the responses. The data reveals a concerning trend, with over one-quarter of respondents feeling that they are "never" treated with humanity and an additional 30.6% experiencing this only "sometimes." This indicates that many displaced persons face dehumanizing treatment, likely in the form of discrimination, neglect, or exclusion from social and economic participation. These findings emphasize the need for interventions to promote dignity, respect, and inclusion for internally displaced persons.

A majority of respondents (64.4%) indicated they "never" experienced arbitrary arrest and detention without trial, and 18.4% reported "always" being free from this form of oppression. Smaller groups chose "hardly" (4.8%), "sometimes" (6.6%), and "often" (5.7%). The chi-square p-value (<0.001) shows a statistically significant distribution. The findings suggest that most respondents feel free from arbitrary arrest and detention, with nearly two-thirds selecting "never." However, approximately 35.6% of respondents expressed varying degrees of concern, indicating that instances of arbitrary arrest or detention may still occur. These cases likely reflect weaknesses in law enforcement practices or systemic discrimination, where displaced persons are unfairly targeted due to their vulnerable status or social stigma.

Impacts of Displacement

The study uncovered significant and multifaceted impacts of internal displacement on affected individuals and communities in South Africa. These impacts were grouped into several categories, including psychosocial effects, economic challenges, social disruptions, and governance-related issues, which together illustrate the profound and far-reaching consequences of displacement.

Psychosocial Impacts

The emotional and psychological toll of displacement emerged as one of the most profound impacts on respondents. Many displaced persons reported ongoing trauma stemming from the sudden loss of their homes and possessions, often in the context of catastrophic events such as floods or fires. Respondents frequently described feelings of hopelessness, anxiety, and depression, compounded by their precarious living conditions. The lack of a sense of safety in resettlement areas exacerbated these emotions, with some individuals recounting sleepless nights due to fears of violence or future disasters.

Children, in particular, were identified as being highly vulnerable to the psychosocial effects of displacement. Disrupted routines, such as interrupted schooling and the loss of familiar surroundings, often led to behavioral changes, including withdrawal, difficulty concentrating, and heightened anxiety. Adults also faced significant challenges in adapting to new environments, with many expressing a sense of alienation and loss of identity as they struggled to rebuild their lives in unfamiliar and often hostile settings.

Economic Impacts

Displacement had a devastating effect on the economic stability of respondents. For many, the loss of homes also meant the loss of livelihoods, particularly for individuals who relied on home-based businesses or proximity to specific employment opportunities. Unemployment was a recurring issue, with 36% of respondents reporting they were unable to secure a stable income after displacement. Those who were employed often experienced reduced earnings, as they struggled to find work in new locations or faced long commutes to previous workplaces.

The economic strain was further compounded by the financial burden of rebuilding. Respondents described the high costs of replacing lost possessions, securing alternative housing, and meeting basic needs, such as food and transportation. Many displaced persons reported borrowing money or depleting their savings to cover these expenses, leaving them trapped in cycles of debt and economic insecurity.

The financial burden of supporting dependents added another layer of complexity. Most respondents reported being responsible for children, elderly relatives, or other family members, which intensified their economic vulnerability. For women, who often bore the dual responsibility of caregiving and earning income, the economic impacts of displacement were particularly pronounced.

Social Impacts

Displacement also disrupted social structures and community networks, which are critical for emotional support and resilience. Many respondents described feeling isolated in their new environments, as they were separated from friends, neighbors, and extended family members. This loss of social cohesion left displaced individuals feeling unsupported and vulnerable.

The breakdown of community ties also had implications for collective action and advocacy. Respondents noted that their displacement often made it difficult to organize and demand better living conditions, as they were scattered across resettlement areas with little opportunity to connect with others who shared their struggles.

The impact on children's education was another significant social consequence. Many families reported that displacement disrupted their children's schooling, either because they were forced to move far from schools or because they could no longer afford associated costs such as uniforms, transportation, and school fees. This disruption threatened to perpetuate cycles of poverty and inequality, as children missed out on critical learning opportunities.

Safety and Security Impacts

A recurring theme among respondents was the heightened sense of insecurity in resettlement areas. Many displaced persons reported increased exposure to crime, including theft, robbery, and gender-based violence. Women and children were particularly vulnerable, with several respondents recounting incidents of harassment and abuse in overcrowded shelters or temporary housing.

The lack of effective law enforcement and security measures in resettlement areas further exacerbated these concerns. Respondents frequently criticized the absence of police patrols or rapid responses to incidents, leaving them to fend for themselves in the face of threats. This sense of insecurity undermined their ability to adapt and recover, as they lived in constant fear for their safety.

Governance and Service Delivery Challenges

Displacement exposed significant gaps in governance and service delivery, which compounded the hardships faced by affected individuals. Respondents expressed frustration with the delays in providing promised Reconstruction and Development Programme (RDP) housing, noting that many had waited years for permanent accommodation. In the interim, they were forced to live in overcrowded shelters or informal settlements, which often lacked basic services such as clean water, sanitation, and electricity.

The lack of effective disaster response and recovery plans further highlighted governance failures. Many respondents described feeling abandoned by authorities during and after displacement events, with little to no support provided for evacuation, temporary housing, or long-term recovery. These governance deficits not only hindered recovery efforts but also eroded trust in public institutions, leaving displaced individuals feeling disillusioned and marginalized.

Cumulative Impacts of Displacement

The study revealed that the impacts of displacement often compounded one another, creating a cycle of vulnerability and hardship. For instance, respondents who lost their homes to flooding also faced economic instability due to job loss, as well as emotional distress from the trauma of the disaster. Similarly, individuals who fled violence often found themselves in unsafe resettlement areas where they were exposed to further threats, exacerbating their sense of insecurity.

These cumulative impacts underscore the interconnected nature of the challenges faced by displaced persons. The combination of economic hardship, social isolation, and governance failures created significant barriers to recovery, leaving many respondents unable to rebuild their lives or achieve stability.

5.4 Qualitative Insights from the interviews on the lived experiences of IDPs

The qualitative findings reveal the human dimensions behind the statistical patterns.

Trauma and Psychosocial Impact

Displacement is associated with profound emotional distress, including anxiety, depression, and loss of identity. Children are particularly affected, experiencing disruptions in education and social development.

Economic Disruption

Loss of livelihoods and unemployment create long-term economic insecurity, often forcing individuals into cycles of poverty and dependence.

Social Disintegration

Displacement disrupts community networks, reducing social support and collective resilience.

Insecurity and Vulnerability

Persistent exposure to crime and violence in resettlement areas undermines recovery and adaptation. The findings demonstrate that internal displacement in South Africa is a multidimensional human rights crisis shaped by the interaction of environmental, social, and governance factors.

While constitutional protections provide a strong normative framework, their uneven implementation reveals systemic challenges in translating rights into lived realities. The persistence of inequality, inadequate service delivery, and climate vulnerability underscores the need for integrated and context-specific interventions.

5.6 Conclusion and Policy Implications

Addressing internal displacement in South Africa requires a comprehensive and rights-based approach that integrates climate resilience, social protection, and governance reform.

Key priorities include:

1. Strengthening disaster risk reduction and climate adaptation strategies.
2. Improving housing delivery and service provision.
3. Enhancing security and protection mechanisms.
4. Supporting livelihoods and economic inclusion.
5. Promoting community-based and collaborative interventions.

Ultimately, displacement must be understood not only as a humanitarian issue but as a systemic challenge requiring long-term structural transformation.

CHAPTER 6

Nigeria: Violence, Crime, and Insecurity

Abstract

This chapter examines the human rights experiences of internally displaced persons (IDPs) in Nigeria within the context of violence, organized crime, and inter-communal conflict. Drawing on a mixed-methods approach that integrates quantitative survey data and qualitative interviews, the chapter analyzes how civic freedoms, socio-economic rights, equality, protection, and personal security are experienced among displaced populations in Niger, Kaduna, and Edo States. Anchored in a rights-based and Africa-centered theoretical framework, the findings reveal that displacement in Nigeria constitutes a deeply structural human rights crisis shaped by political instability, ethno-religious tensions, and governance deficits. The results further demonstrate that human rights experiences are not uniform but are significantly mediated by demographic factors such as age, education, and employment status. Comparative insights situate Nigeria within broader African displacement dynamics, highlighting both shared patterns and context-specific drivers.

Keywords: Internal displacement, human rights, Nigeria, conflict, communal violence, governance

6.1 Introduction

Building on the analysis of climate and socio-economic displacement in South Africa, this chapter examines Nigeria, where internal displacement is predominantly driven by violence, organized crime, insurgency, and communal conflict.

This chapter completes the trilogy of case studies by introducing a context in which displacement is shaped by both state fragility and non-state violence, including banditry, insurgency, and ethno-religious tensions. In contrast to Cameroon's political conflict and South Africa's environmental vulnerabilities, Nigeria represents a convergence of security, governance, and structural inequality challenges.

The chapter reinforces key themes emerging from the previous cases—particularly the interdependence of human rights and the role of structural inequalities—while also highlighting the scale and intensity of displacement in highly volatile environments.

Having examined these three distinct yet interconnected contexts, the next chapter synthesizes the findings to develop a comparative framework and policy agenda for Sub-Saharan Africa.

Internal displacement in Nigeria is predominantly driven by human-induced factors, including organized violence, insurgency, and inter-communal conflict. Unlike environmental displacement, which is often sudden and episodic, conflict-induced displacement reflects prolonged structural instability and entrenched socio-political tensions.

Nigeria remains one of the most affected countries globally, with millions displaced by violence linked to insurgency, banditry, and communal conflicts. These forms of violence are rooted in complex interactions between political exclusion, resource competition, religious divisions, and historical inequalities.

This chapter examines the lived experiences of IDPs in Nigeria, focusing on how displacement affects the realization of human rights. It adopts a multidisciplinary framework that integrates legal, socio-economic, and Africa-centered perspectives to analyze both the structural drivers and lived realities of displacement.

6.2 Drivers of Displacement in Nigeria

Studies on the phenomenon of internal displacement in Nigeria have extensively dwelt on violence and organized criminality as the fundamental causes of the scourge (Aondover et al., 2025; Adeola, 2021; Adesina et al., 2020; Dirikgil, 2022; Dunn, 2018; Ekezie, 2022). This unfortunate connection is corroborated by data from the Internal Displacement Monitoring Center (IDMC), which puts the number of people displaced in Nigeria as a result of violent crime at over three million (IDMC, 2024). Further engagement with literature on the nature of organized violent crimes in Nigeria reveals multiple underlying causes, such as political intolerance (Hossain & Hossain, 2024), communal conflicts (Anierobi et al., 2024), insurgent attacks by groups such as Boko Haram (Umar et al., 2023), and religious intolerance (Ezegwu & Okoye, 2024).

In their study on political alignment and organized violence in Nigeria, Hossain & Hossain (2024) argue that there is a nexus between political affiliation and the level of organized criminality that causes displacement, harm, and death to many victims. Using data from the 2011 House of Representatives elections in Nigeria, the authors substantiate that the incidences of violence perpetrated by extremist groups against civilians and government officials seem lower in highly contested constituencies that were won by candidates aligned with the political party governing at the national level. Mang and Ehrhardt (2018) further posit that toxic political ideologies, which characterized colonial administrations, sowed the seeds of discord by creating discriminatory tendencies among elites. These arbitrary policies planted the roots of chaos in the Nigerian political landscape by influencing who qualified for political appointments, employment, and access to education.

6.2.1 Communal Conflict and Resource Competition

Communal conflicts—particularly farmer-herder clashes—represent a major driver of displacement. These conflicts are often rooted in competition over land and resources, compounded by ethnic and religious divisions. Communal conflicts differ from politically engendered violence in the sense that the differences between the opposing parties are rooted in the communities to which they belong. In essence, people are drawn into the conflict based on their loyalty to a certain community, and this sense of belonging attracts hostility from people whose allegiance is with the other community. Aondover et al. (2025) assert that communal violence accounts for 79.7% of internally displaced persons in Taraba State. In Bauchi State, the percentage is equally high at 55.4%. While many community groups are identified along geographical and ethnic lines, Madueke (2019) points out factors such as age groups, education, occupation, and other situational affiliations. In the Nigerian context, some common triggers of communal conflicts have been identified as land disputes, land invasions, annexations, and farmer-herder clashes, among others. Further differences come from the fact that most of the farmers are Christians, whereas the herders are predominantly Fulani and Muslims, which generally fuel tensions between the two communities.

6.2.2 Insurgency and Organized Violence

The Boko Haram insurgency has had devastating impacts, displacing millions and destroying livelihoods and infrastructure. The violence disproportionately affects vulnerable populations, particularly women and children. The group is well known for its atrocities in Nigeria and beyond (Aondover et al., 2025). It is quite active in parts of northeastern Nigeria, where it has terrorized millions of people, particularly peasant farmers, fishermen, teachers, women, children, politicians, clerics, traders, professionals, and security personnel. Women and children have borne the brunt of their attacks and constitute approximately 80% of IDPs, largely due to their vulnerability (Mojaye & Msughter, 2022). According to the United Nations Development Programme (UNDP, 2017), the Islamic insurgency, which started in 2009, has disrupted the social, economic, and institutional fabric of the region. Besides the human cost of the insurgency, there has been a significant impact on physical infrastructure, the disruption of social services, the loss of livelihoods, and the disruption of social cohesion (World Bank, 2016). In essence, the Boko Haram insurgency has not only depleted the available resources in the region but has also exhausted survival strategies and weakened the ability of families to handle shocks over time (Cadre Harmonisé, 2017).

6.2.3 Political and Religious Tensions

Ethno-religious divisions and political exclusion have intensified conflict dynamics. Perceived inequalities in resource allocation and governance contribute to mistrust and violence. Nigeria is an ethno-cultural melting pot with over 250 ethnic groups, about 510 identifiable languages, and three dominant religious practices, namely Islam, Christianity, and traditional practices (Ezegwu & Okoye, 2024).

However, religious extremism has often spilt into the political space. Adenuga et al., (2023) define ethno-religious conflicts as confrontations in which opposing parties are motivated by religious differences. In the context of Nigeria, these conflicts have largely been between the Muslim-dominated ruling Northern/Hausa/Fulani groups and the Christian-dominated South-East/Igbo groups (Adenuga et al. 2022). One point of contention has been attempts to impose the Sharia Legal Code in the Northern States dominated by the Muslim population (Levan, 2015; Osaghae & Suberu, 2005). The Christian population, which is in the minority in these regions, has resisted the institutionalization of Sharia law.

Moreover, perceived political bias and unfair allocation of resources based on religious affiliation have created suspicion, increased the trust deficit, and heightened religious tensions. For instance, when the federal government of Nigeria instituted the Rural Grazing Area (RUGA) policy in 2019, it was largely rejected and resisted by Christians who form the majority in the South and other ethnic minorities in the North, who believed it favored the Hausa/Fulani ethnic group (Ademola, 2020; Adenuga, 2022; Chukwuma, 2020; Ele, 2020). It is evident from this case, and other instances, that mistrust and perceived bias in the allocation of resources based on ethnic and religious identities have engendered hostilities and violence (Horowitz, 1985).

The repercussions of these hostilities have been disastrous, as Aondover et al. (2025) allude to 2811 incidences of ethnic conflict with 18,132 fatalities, 3703 incidences of religious conflict with 29,957 fatalities, and 117 incidences of ethnoreligious conflict with 2420 fatalities between 2019 and 2021. The impacts of these conflicts are also evident in the large number of internally displaced persons in Nigeria.

6.2.4 Crime, Banditry, and Insecurity

Banditry, kidnapping, and armed robbery have emerged as significant drivers of displacement, particularly in northern Nigeria. These forms of criminal violence create pervasive fear and insecurity, forcing communities to flee.

6.3 Contextualizing the IDP Situation in Nigeria

The Internal Displacement Monitoring Center (IDMC) puts the number of internally displaced people in the world at 59.1 million (IDMC, 2022). Even more disturbing is the fact that the global report on internal displacement reveals that more than half of internal displacement (38 million) only occurred in 2021, with 14.4 million (38%) of forced migrations prompted by conflicts and violence and 23.7 million (62%) triggered by disasters (IDMC, 2022). These figures present a bleak picture considering the unpredictable conditions faced by IDPs who are often forced out of their livelihoods, and futile global efforts are made to curb the scourge of internal displacement. The UNHCR asserts that the number of people who flee from their homes in search of refuge within the borders of their country is significantly higher than those who cross national borders as refugees or asylum seekers (UNHCR 2021). From a regional perspective, Sub-Saharan Africa was among the worst affected by internal displacements in 2021, with 11,558,000 people forcibly displaced by conflicts and violence and 2,554,000 triggered by disasters (IDMC, 2022). This number accounts for 37.1% of all IDPs in 2021, making Sub-Saharan Africa second only to East Asia and the Pacific (37.6%) in the world (IDMC, 2022).

In the context of Nigeria, the recorded number of IDPs stood at 2.7 million in 2020 (Statista 2022). However, this number increased by 400,000 in 2021, with disasters accounting for the displacement of

24,000 people and 376,000 forcibly removed by violence and conflict (IDMC 2022). The Boko Haram insurgency is estimated to account for the forced displacement of 3.9 million people in Nigeria within the last decade, with 2.1 million of these living as IDPs (International Organization for Migration (IOM) 2021; UNHCR 2021). Most victims of this armed conflict have been residents of states in the northern part of Nigeria, such as Borno, Yobe, and Adamawa (Dunn et al. 2018). Many survivors of these armed attacks and kidnappings tend to flee to relatively safer regions where they either live in camps or among community members (UNHCR 2021).

Crawford et al. (2015) observed that once displaced for more than six months, IDPs tend to live in displacement for longer periods of more than three years. Following the same line of thought, Mubarak et al. (2016) and Siriwardhana et al. (2015) assert that the trauma experienced by IDPs as a result of the forced displacement from their homes, loss of their livelihoods, and separation from their families often results in increased incidents of diseases, food insecurity, and mental health challenges. These challenges are often exacerbated by the prolonged stay away from their home environment (Roberts et al. 2009). Therefore, Ekezie (2022) argues that recent efforts to assist IDPs have shifted from settling them in camps to providing them with opportunities for sustainable livelihoods. However, Adesina et al. (2020) raise an important concern regarding the large number of IDPs who do not migrate to camps but rather settle among local residents and thus pose unique challenges in being identified. Despite the increasing research interest in the plight of IDPs, Blanchet et al. (2017) and Rass et al. (2020) lament the paucity of studies exploring the views of IDPs. This study, therefore, aims to contribute to closing these research gaps by exploring the perceptions of IDPs living among local residents in the states of Niger, Kaduna, and Edo regarding their experience of various human rights provisions. The following questions are central to this study:

- Who are the IDPs in Niger, Kaduna, and Edo states?
- What are the experiences of the IDPS with regard to their basic human rights?
- What are the key motivations/aspirations among the IDPs?
- How can the human rights needs of the IDPs be addressed?

The geopolitical situation of Kaduna, Niger, and Edo states, where the field work for this study was conducted, renders them relatively peaceful and attractive to IDPs as they are more centrally located and away from the main battlegrounds such as Borno, Adamawa, Yobe, Benue, Nasarawa, Plateau, Kaduna, Kano, Sokoto, Katsina, and Zamfara. Once out of the conflict zones, many IDPs settle in structured environments, such as camps, where there is relatively easy access to humanitarian assistance (Olanrewaju et al., 2019), while others settle among host community members (Ekezie, 2022). Participants in this study were IDPs who had blended into the community and had largely been ignored by previous studies (Ibrahim, 2019; Obiefuna & Adams, 2021).

6.4 Quantitative Findings: Human Rights Dimensions

6.4.1 Demographic Profile and Structural Vulnerability

The 700 questionnaires distributed to internally displaced persons in Niger, Kaduna, and Edo states in Nigeria yielded a response rate of 83.4%, with 584 duly completed responses returned.

The descriptive results presented in Table 6.1 reveal the profiles of the respondents who participated in this study.

Table 6.1. Demographic characteristics of respondents

Variable	Description	Frequency	Percentage
Location of IDPs	Niger state	146	25
	Kaduna State	258	44
	Edo State	180	31
Origin of IDPs	Zamfara State	43	7
	Plateau State	16	3
	Kebbi State	12	2
	Sokoto State	19	3
	Niger State	56	10
	Kaduna State	191	33
	Borno State	188	32
	Adamawa State	53	10
Reasons for displacement	Flooding	79	14
	War	326	56
	Fire	19	3
	Kidnapping	53	9
	Banditry	93	16
	Herdsmen and farmers' conflict	12	2
Gender	Male	293	50.2
	Female	291	49.8
Age	18 - 25	193	33
	26 – 35	134	22
	36 – 45	149	26
	46 – 55	80	14
	56 – 65	23	4
	65+	5	1

Employment status	Unemployed	291	49.8
	Self-employed	169	28.9
	Government employee	55	9.4
	Private sector employee	69	11.9
Education status	No formal education	108	18.5
	Primary school	129	22.1
	Pre-University	110	18.8
	University	44	7.5
	National Diploma	70	12
	First degree	96	16.4
	Post graduate	27	4.7

Source: Author, 2026

The findings presented in Table 6.1 reveal high levels of unemployment, low educational attainment, and a youthful population among IDPs. These factors significantly influence access to rights and economic stability, reinforcing patterns of vulnerability. These factors provide essential context for understanding variations in experiences, perceptions, and challenges faced by internally displaced persons (IDPs) in Nigeria. The analysis highlights demographic patterns that influence access to rights, economic stability, and social integration.

The majority (n = 486, 83.2%) of respondents indicated that they had been displaced due to communal violence, highlighting the severe impact of conflict on forced migration. A smaller proportion were displaced by flooding (n = 98, 16.8%). These figures underscore the dominance of conflict as the primary driver of displacement among the surveyed population.

The sample consisted of 293 males (50.2%) and 291 females (49.8%) (p = 0.934), indicating an almost equal gender distribution among the respondents. This balanced representation provides a perspective on the experiences of both men and women, allowing for a balanced analysis of gender-related differences in displacement, access to rights, and socio-economic challenges.

Findings on the Human Rights Variables

A summary of the findings on the respondents' perceptions of the Human rights variables is presented in Table 6.2 below.

Table 6.2 Perceived Human Rights services received by respondents.

Frequency of service		Never		Hardly		Sometimes		Often		Always		
Human Rights attributes		Count	%	Count	%	Count	%	Count	%	Count	N %	Chi-Square p-value
You feel free to practice your culture without fear (B1)	B1	58	9.9	49	8.4	122	20.9	84	14.4	271	46.4	<0.001
You feel free to practice your religion without fear (B2)	B2	63	10.8	35	6.0	90	15.4	59	10.1	337	57.7	<0.001
You feel free to speak your language without fear (B3)	B3	76	13.0	35	6.0	107	18.3	64	11.0	302	51.7	<0.001
You have a right to vote during elections (B4)	B4	62	10.6	30	5.1	75	12.8	84	14.4	333	57.0	<0.001
Police and security forces worked hard to assist you when you were still in your home (D1)	D1	167	28.6	99	17.0	194	33.2	62	10.6	62	10.6	<0.001
Police and security assist you every time you call for help (D2)	D2	147	25.2	85	14.6	143	24.5	69	11.8	140	24.0	<0.001
You have been treated equally to everyone in this community (D3)	D3	89	15.2	62	10.6	156	26.7	65	11.1	212	36.3	<0.001
You feel free to walk around and talk without fear (D4)	D4	76	13.0	58	9.9	143	24.5	81	13.9	226	38.7	<0.001
You have not been treated as a slave (E1)	E1	281	48.1	65	11.1	112	19.2	39	6.7	87	14.9	<0.001
People have not treated you as if you are not a human being (E2)	E2	229	39.2	71	12.2	152	26.0	45	7.7	87	14.9	<0.001
You have not been arrested and detained without trial (E3)	E3	356	61.0	50	8.6	71	12.2	34	5.8	73	12.5	<0.001
You have space to do your private and personal things without people watching you (F1)	F1	77	13.2	76	13.0	199	34.1	91	15.6	141	24.1	<0.001
You live in a safe and comfortable house where you do not fear (F2)	F2	59	10.1	85	14.6	134	22.9	116	19.9	190	32.5	<0.001
You feel that your life is not in danger in this community (F3)	F3	143	24.5	93	15.9	113	19.3	72	12.3	163	27.9	<0.001

While many respondents reported some degree of cultural and religious freedom, political participation remains uneven. Restrictions on voting and civic engagement reflect broader governance challenges. Access to food, water, healthcare, and education remains inconsistent, with widespread deprivation reported. These findings underscore the systemic nature of socio-economic inequalities among displaced populations.

Perceptions of law enforcement were largely negative, with many respondents reporting limited assistance from police and security forces. Experiences of discrimination and unequal treatment were also common. High levels of perceived exploitation, dehumanization, and arbitrary detention highlight serious violations of human dignity and personal liberty. Safety and privacy remain significant concerns, with many respondents reporting insecurity in their living environments. Overcrowding and inadequate housing exacerbate these challenges.

6.5 Interconnected Human Rights attributes based on Structural Equation Modeling (SEM)

The SEM analysis (Figure 6.1) confirms the interdependence of human rights dimensions, demonstrating that:

- Economic stability enhances civic participation.
- Equality and protection strengthen social inclusion.
- Oppression undermines all other rights.
- Security is foundational to human dignity and well-being.

These results indicate that the SEM model exhibits good construct validity and reliability, reinforcing its suitability for analyzing latent relationships between human rights dimensions among internally displaced persons (IDPs). The robust reliability and validity measures provide a solid foundation for drawing meaningful insights from the data.

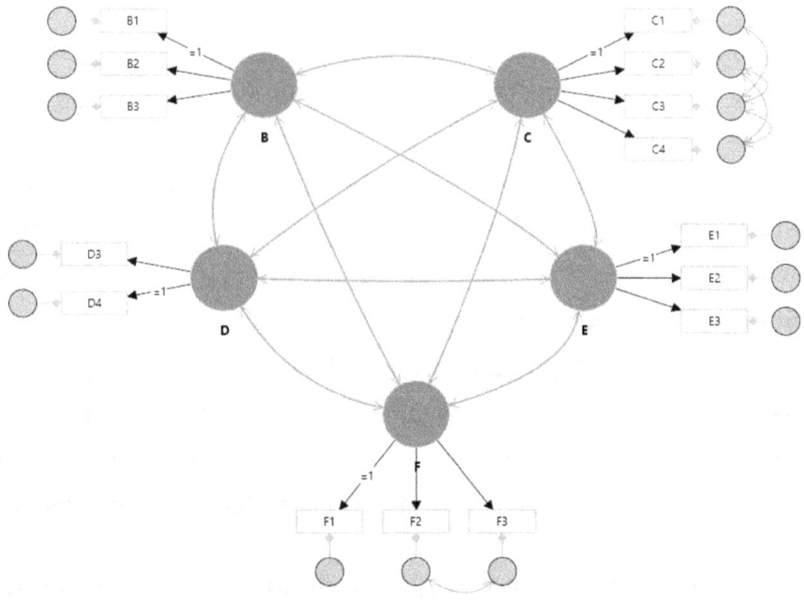

Figure 6.1 Factor Correlations of Human Rights Variables

Factor correlations illustrate the strength and direction of relationships among the model's constructs. The results provide insights into how different dimensions of human rights experiences among internally displaced persons (IDPs) are interrelated.

- **Fundamental Economic and Social Rights (C) → Civic and Political Freedoms (B):** ($r = 0.6241$, $p < 0.001$) – A strong positive correlation suggests that improved economic and social rights enhance civic and political freedoms.

- **Equality and Protection Rights (D) → Civic and Political Freedoms (B):** ($r = 0.9503$, $p < 0.001$) – A very strong positive correlation, indicating that increased legal protections and equality contribute significantly to political and civic engagement.
- **Equality and Protection Rights (D) → Fundamental Economic and Social Rights (C):** ($r = 0.6167$, $p < 0.001$) – A moderate-to-strong positive correlation, confirming that economic security and legal protections are closely tied.
- **Freedom from Oppression (E) → Civic and Political Freedoms (B):** ($r = -0.6770$, $p < 0.001$) – A significant negative correlation, suggesting that higher levels of oppression limit civic and political freedoms.
- **Freedom from Oppression (E) → Fundamental Economic and Social Rights (C):** ($r = -0.4062$, $p < 0.001$) – A moderate negative correlation, implying that economic well-being is negatively impacted by oppression.
- **Freedom from Oppression (E) → Equality and Protection Rights (D):** ($r = -0.6960$, $p < 0.001$) – A strong negative correlation, indicating that oppression undermines legal protections and equality.
- **Security and Privacy (F) → Civic and Political Freedoms (B):** ($r = 0.8701$, $p < 0.001$) – A strong positive correlation, demonstrating that increased security and privacy promote civic and political engagement.
- **Security and Privacy (F) → Fundamental Economic and Social Rights (C):** ($r = 0.7248$, $p < 0.001$) – A strong positive correlation, confirming that security enhances economic stability.

- **Security and Privacy (F) → Equality and Protection Rights (D):** ($r = 0.8554$, $p < 0.001$) – A strong positive correlation, reinforcing the importance of security in ensuring legal protections and equality.
- **Security and Privacy (F) → Freedom from Oppression (E):** ($r = -0.6302$, $p < 0.001$) – A significant negative correlation, suggesting that greater security and privacy reduce experiences of oppression.

These correlations highlight systemic relationships among human rights dimensions: increased security, legal protections, and economic rights contribute positively to civic freedoms, while oppression negatively affects all dimensions. Biographical factors, such as age, education, and employment, significantly mediate these relationships, highlighting the importance of targeted interventions.

6.6 Qualitative Insights: Human Rights Realities of Internally Displaced Persons

The qualitative phase of the study in Nigeria involved thirty (30) interviews with purposively selected respondents in management or leadership positions among internally displaced persons in Niger State, Kaduna State, and Edo State. The thirty interviews were conducted with ten IDPs purposively selected in each of the purposively selected states. For convenience and anonymity, the interviewees were coded W1–W30. The cluster map in Figure 6.2 below was generated from the interview transcripts.

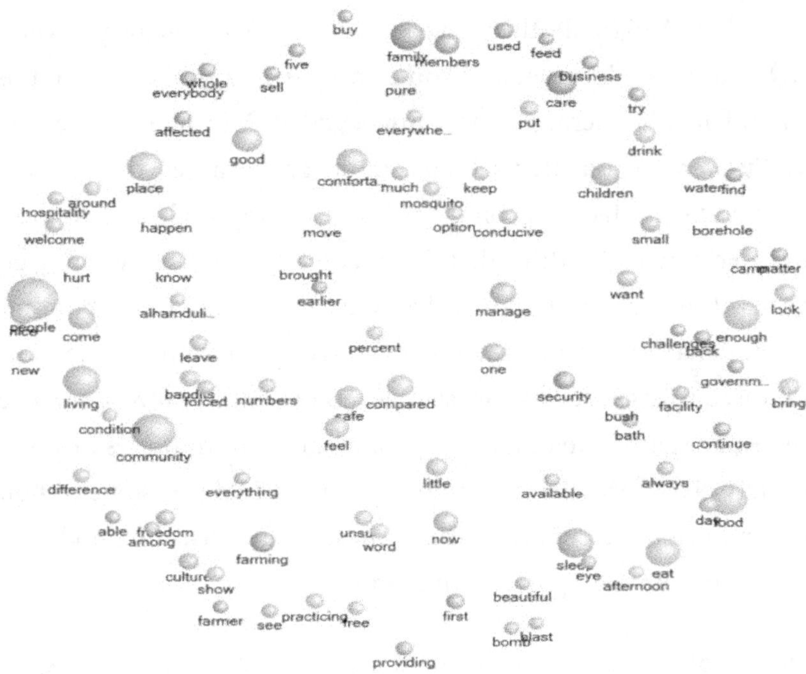

Figure 6.2 Cluster map of interviews conducted with IDPs in Nigeria

The following themes were generated from the transcribed interviews:

Conditions Forcing People to Flee from Their Homes and Communities

Analysis of the qualitative data from the interviews produced the first primary subtheme on the conditions forcing people to become internally displaced. The insecurity and fear created by bandits and armed robbers emerged as a prominent cause of displacement. Respondents recounted horrific stories of the agony they encountered from bandits and armed robbers. Bandits attacked their communities, looting food and livestock, and causing loss of life. In the words of respondent W16 (male, thirty-six years old), "We are facing you know, the bandits, herds' men, and sometimes armed robbers." Another respondent W22 (female, thirty-nine), added, "Hmm, that question, bandits were the one that send us out of communities, they came in their numbers, attack our communities, took away food, our livestock." An elderly man W6 (fifty-three), lamented how things actually got worse, "The bandits and lot of lives were lost, we had to run for our lives and that is what brought us here." It is evident from the interviews that insecurity caused by excessive levels of banditry forced many of the respondents to abandon their homes and communities in search of safety elsewhere. Besides the high levels of robbery, some respondents reported incidents of kidnappings, explosions, and flooding as the reasons for fleeing in search of safety.

Impacts of Internal Displacement on Affected Persons in Nigeria

Having explored the tragic circumstances that triggered the displacement of the respondents, the focus of the discussions shifted to how internal displacement has affected their living conditions. The first sub-theme that emerged here was the grave impact that internal displacement has on families and communities in general. It was evident that multiple families had been uprooted from their homes and left destitute as they struggled for basic necessities of life, such as shelter, food, and security. Family units including spouses, children, and other relations were forced to flee in different directions. One respondent W8 (female aged forty-three), recounted the final moments when the family was torn apart, "Well, all five of us. Five of my family members, myself, and my husband and three of our children were affected. We all got up quickly and ran in separate [different] directions in the dark." Still visibly shaken by the tragic events, respondent W29 (male, aged forty-nine), lamented in a soft tone, "So all our family members we don't even know where they are now, everybody is scattered, they don't know where we are at the moment."

Another prominent sub-theme was the impact of the violence on neighbors and the entire community. Multiple communities fled their areas in search of refuge wherever they could find safety. Respondent W26 (male, aged forty-two), emotionally described the chaotic scenes that ensued when the intruders attacked their village, "All our communities [they] fled [while] screaming. Unfortunately, some people didn't make it. They died in the darkness. Now, we are taking refuge in this place." Corroborating the scale of the tragic circumstances and displacement, respondent W2 (female, aged thirty-two), added that "All of the people living around were affected by this terrible situation, so it was just something that we can't forget. All our village people were in this tragic incident."

The socio-economic impacts of internal displacement also emerged as a prominent theme from the interviews. Participants expressed frustration at the loss of their livelihoods and the fact that they currently live on handouts from sympathizers. One respondent W13 (female, thirty-four), took a deep breath and explained, "I am a farmer. We were doing farming too." Another female participant W25 (aged thirty-four), supported the assertion by saying, "I was selling farm produce from my husband's farm. He was able to farm yam, maize, and melon." Still, another female respondent W5 (aged thirty-three), indicated, "I do trading. I buy and sell cassavas and yams but now there is no market."

The social responsibility sub-theme focused largely on the care that respondents had over younger or elderly family members. There was a large degree of familial responsibility and care. This extended to siblings, mother, spouse, and children. Despite facing various challenges, respondents remained dedicated to ensuring their family members' daily needs were met. For some, being the eldest in the household also required that they exercise leadership and nurturing qualities. Respondent W11 (female, aged thirty-two) explained, "I wasn't taking care of only myself, I was taking care of my husband and my children. Whatever profit I get from my small business, I try to use the profit to take care of my children, feeding them. I also support my husband to take of my family." Similar sentiments were shared by another respondent W17 (male, aged thirty-eight), who said, "Well, I take care of my family members because my parents are old."

The last major sub-theme discussed in the interviews focused on the current living conditions and the respect for basic human rights provisions among internally displaced persons in their new places of residence. There were mixed reactions to this, indicating both good and poor conditions. However, many deficiencies were pointed out in the living conditions of the respondents. Some respondents struggled to sleep at night due to persistent thoughts and memories of past traumatic experiences. Their sleep was inconsistent with frequent awakenings due to the contrast between their current situation and their past hardships. Respondent W10 (male, aged forty-one), said, "I don't sleep that well at night, I don't sleep well. I sleep with my one eye open because the thoughts of what we experienced where we came is always with me. Oh, I hope they will not [come] here again. Sleep small, wake up small, then continue sleep. We pray hoping for a better day."

Other respondents lamented that mosquitoes were a constant menace and that, despite attempts to mitigate mosquito infestations with nets, they still faced difficulties. They expressed dissatisfaction with the lack of comfort and freedom in their living spaces due to this. In the words of one respondent W13 (female, aged thirty-one),

"I'll keep on saying we are managing here because we don't have [any] options. The comfort is say, forty percent. Mosquitoes everywhere, you cannot freely do whatever you want. If we put mosquito nets sometimes it's not enough."

Insecurity was identified as one of the major concerns of internally displaced persons. Many respondents emphasized that security must be improved in the current location to ensure safety and well-being. Some respondents appealed to the government for assistance in addressing security issues. Respondent W5 (female, aged twenty-eight), appealed to the government, saying, "It's not conducive here. We are pleading [with] the government to find a lasting solution to these security challenges." In support of this view, a male respondent W16 (aged fifty-one), added, "We are pleading that the government provides us with security or help us to go back; yes, we want to go back; that is our major problem, to go back to our communities."

The general perspective among the respondents is that food rations are insufficient. Whilst acknowledging that the government and some organizations donate food parcels to internally displaced persons, some respondents decry the fact that food had to be shared among families and, in some instances, children had to be prioritized over adults. In the words of respondent W4 (female, aged thirty-three), "If we can get more food. some organizations come to donate food for us but the food is not enough because the food that they will bring they will share it household by household, which is not enough, before you know it has finished." However, some respondents expressed concern with the lack of variety in the meals. Receiving a bag of rice, for example, was a kind gesture, but it was essential to supplement it with other varieties of food. At this point, respondent W25 (male, aged thirty-seven), interjected, "Food is very expensive and as I don't have any job here, it's tough like pulling a tooth."

Unlike the sub-theme of food, where respondents expressed multiple shortcomings that required attention, water provision received mixed reviews, with some respondents expressing satisfaction with the quality and quantity of water, while others had a number of concerns. One respondent W22 (female, aged thirty-six), remarked, “The water is also pure because it’s always treated before you drink and there’s good supply of water here.” However, respondent W13 (female, aged forty-one), expressed concern, saying, “There’s a borehole in this camp but there’s not enough because everyone wants water. Sometimes we go to the community here to go and look for water. We have a borehole here that we managing.” Worse conditions were reported where one respondent W13 (female, aged thirty-eight), said, “The water has color and is having taste but sometimes the NGO people bring some kind of purification for us to put in the water before we can drink it.”

Other sub-themes covered in the interviews are summarized in Table 6.7 below:

Table 6.3 Sub-theme analysis from interviews with respondents.

Sub-theme	**Respondents' Perception**	**Direct Quotation**
Toilet and bath (ablution) facilities.	The lack of adequate toilet facilities is a pressing challenge for some respondents, leading to challenges in maintaining hygiene and privacy. Due to insufficient facilities, children often resort to defecating in nearby bushes within the camp, posing health and safety risks. Additionally, limited bathing facilities force respondents to seek alternative locations for bathing.	"The toilet facilities are not enough. Sometimes our children go to the bush within the camp, and they just defecate there." (W7, female aged thirty-eight). "Eh, sometimes when we want to bath, you have [to] wait or you look for one corner to go and bath. No, not enough toilet facilities." (W1, male, aged fifty-two).
Healthcare	Some camps do not have medical facilities; hence, people needing medical attention have to go to other communities. The makeshift clinic within the camp lacks adequate resources to handle medical emergencies, particularly for sick children.	"The makeshift clinic they put here, if our children are sick they cannot be treated there. We have to start looking out [of] the camp to go and find healthcare. The facility here is not enough." (W20, female, aged thirty-three).

Obtaining Income	Some respondents reported that they are struggling to find jobs in order to earn income. Thus, compromising their ability to provide for their families.	"I'm struggling to earn a living and provide for the family." (W17, male, aged forty). "So I also trade here, I buy and sell so from there I make money to feed my family." (W29, Female, aged thirty-six).
Hospitality	There is a generally positive perception of the friendliness of the local community. The IDPs received help to settle in, find food and other basic necessities. This initial act of kindness from the local community reflected compassion and solidarity during challenging times.	"Yeah, Well, when we first came here the people here took pity on us so they offered us food for the meantime." (W30, male, aged forty). "Ermm, I feel it very much free here because the people here are welcoming and hospitable." (W10, female, aged twenty-six). "Well, as I said earlier I feel good because the people around here are nice, they are good people, they don't show any differences to us." (W8, male, aged thirty-four).

Conclusions

The focus of this chapter was to explore the human rights situation of people displaced by organized or rampant crime in selected states in Nigeria. Whilst the previous chapter examined the circumstances of people displaced by floods and other natural phenomena in the Southern African sub-region, notably South Africa, this chapter shifts to human-induced displacement in Nigeria (West African Region). It contributes towards filling the research gap identified in the literature (Adesina et al., 2020; Akpoghome, 2015; Cantor et al., 2021) on the need for further research exploring the living conditions of internally displaced persons in Nigeria.

Demographic insights presented in the quantitative part of this chapter can serve as a guide to policymakers and those planning for support and assistance for internally displaced persons in affected communities. Even though there is near gender parity among the IDPs, this study has revealed that the youthful population (eighteen to twenty-five years) has been disproportionately affected; hence, their needs should be prioritized. The 33% of youth among the displaced respondents is slightly higher than the 23% found in a previous study by Anierobi et al. (2024). However, both figures confirm a relatively high number of young people affected.

The findings demonstrate that internal displacement in Nigeria is a systemic human rights crisis driven by structural violence, governance deficits, and socio-political fragmentation.

The interdependence of rights highlights the need for integrated approaches that address both immediate needs and underlying structural drivers. The role of demographic factors further underscores the importance of targeted and context-specific interventions.

Policy Implications

Addressing internal displacement in Nigeria requires a comprehensive, rights-based approach that prioritizes:

1. Strengthening security and conflict resolution mechanisms.
2. Enhancing access to basic services and livelihoods.
3. Promoting social cohesion and community reintegration.
4. Addressing structural inequalities and governance deficits.
5. Supporting vulnerable groups through targeted interventions.

CHAPTER 7

Toward a Human Rights-informed Internal Displacement Framework for Sub-Saharan Africa

Abstract

This chapter synthesizes findings from the preceding country case studies—Cameroon, South Africa, and Nigeria—to provide a comparative analysis of the human rights experiences of internally displaced persons (IDPs) across diverse African contexts. Drawing on rights-based, capability, human security, and Africa-centered theoretical frameworks, the chapter demonstrates that internal displacement constitutes a multidimensional and systemic human rights crisis shaped by conflict, environmental vulnerability, and structural inequality. While the drivers of displacement vary across the three countries, common patterns emerge in the erosion of civic freedoms, socio-economic deprivation, weak protection systems, and persistent insecurity. The chapter concludes with practical and policy recommendations for addressing human rights gaps at national and regional levels.

Keywords: Internal displacement, human rights, Africa, comparative analysis, policy, governance

7.1 Introduction

Having examined internal displacement across three distinct contexts—conflict in Cameroon, climate and inequality in South

Africa, and violence and crime in Nigeria—this chapter brings these cases together into a comparative analytical framework. The purpose of this chapter is to move beyond country-specific findings and identify common patterns, structural drivers, and policy-relevant insights. It demonstrates that, despite differing triggers, internal displacement across these contexts reflects a shared set of challenges rooted in governance deficits, inequality, and insecurity. This synthesis chapter consolidates the central argument of the book: that internal displacement in Africa is a systemic human rights crisis requiring integrated, rights-based, and context-sensitive responses. The chapter also lays the groundwork for the final section of the book, which translates these insights into practical policy recommendations and actionable strategies for stakeholders.

Internal displacement in Sub-Saharan Africa reflects a convergence of conflict, environmental change, and structural inequality. The preceding chapters have examined these dynamics in Cameroon (conflict-driven displacement), South Africa (climate and socio-economic displacement), and Nigeria (violence and organized crime).

This chapter brings these cases together to identify shared patterns, key divergences, and policy-relevant insights. It moves beyond country-specific analysis to develop a comparative human rights framework that can inform both national and regional responses.

7.2 Comparative Drivers of Internal Displacement

7.2.1 Typologies of Displacement

Across the three countries, displacement is driven by distinct but overlapping factors:

Table 7.1 Dynamic nature of internal displacement in Cameroon, South Africa, and Nigeria.

Country	Primary Driver	Nature of Displacement
Cameroon	Armed conflict	Political and identity-based violence.
South Africa	Climate and inequality	Environmental and socio-economic.
Nigeria	Crime and insurgency	Violent conflict and insecurity.

Despite these differences, all three contexts reveal that displacement is rooted in structural vulnerabilities rather than isolated events.

7.2.2 Structural Drivers

A comparative analysis highlights three underlying drivers common across contexts:

1. Governance deficits—weak institutions and limited state capacity.
2. Inequality and marginalization— socio-economic and spatial disparities.
3. Insecurity and violence—both direct and structural forms.

These findings align with the concept of structural violence (Galtung, 1969), where systemic inequalities produce and sustain human suffering.

7.3 Comparative Human Rights Experiences

7.3.1 Civic and Political Rights

Across all three countries, IDPs experience varying degrees of civic freedom. While cultural and religious expression is often preserved, political participation is consistently constrained, particularly in conflict-affected areas.

This reflects a broader pattern of political exclusion among displaced populations, limiting their ability to influence decisions affecting their lives.

7.3.2 Economic and Social Rights

A common thread across the three cases is widespread deprivation of basic needs, including:

- Food insecurity.
- Limited access to clean water.
- Inadequate healthcare.
- Disrupted education.

These conditions illustrate capability deprivation (Sen, 1999), where individuals lack the resources and opportunities to achieve well-being.

7.3.3 Equality, Protection, and Justice

Perceptions of state protection are generally weak across all contexts. IDPs frequently report:

- Limited assistance from security forces.

- Experiences of discrimination.
- Lack of legal protection.

This highlights a crisis of institutional trust, particularly in fragile and conflict-affected settings.

7.3.4 Security and Human Dignity

Insecurity remains a defining feature of displacement across all three countries. Whether due to armed conflict, crime, or unsafe living conditions, IDPs face ongoing threats to their safety and dignity.

The human security framework (UNDP, 1994) is particularly relevant here, as it captures the multidimensional nature of insecurity experienced by IDPs.

7.4 Interdependence of Human Rights

A key finding across all three case studies is the interconnected nature of human rights:

- Civic freedoms enable economic participation.
- Economic stability enhances security.
- Security reduces vulnerability to oppression.

Conversely:

- Oppression undermines all other rights.
- Insecurity disrupts economic and social systems.
- Inequality limits access to protection.

This reinforces the principle of the indivisibility of human rights, central to international human rights law.

7.5 Intersectionality and Differential Vulnerability

Across all contexts, human rights experiences are shaped by demographic factors:

- Gender: Women face heightened risks of exploitation and economic exclusion.
- Age: Youth are more mobile but economically vulnerable.
- Education: Higher education improves access to opportunities and rights awareness.
- Employment: Economic stability enhances protection and reduces vulnerability.

These findings underscore the importance of intersectional policy approaches.

7.6 Conceptual Model for Internal Displacement in Africa

The internal displacement situation covered in this book can be summarised using the model presented in Figure 7.3 below.

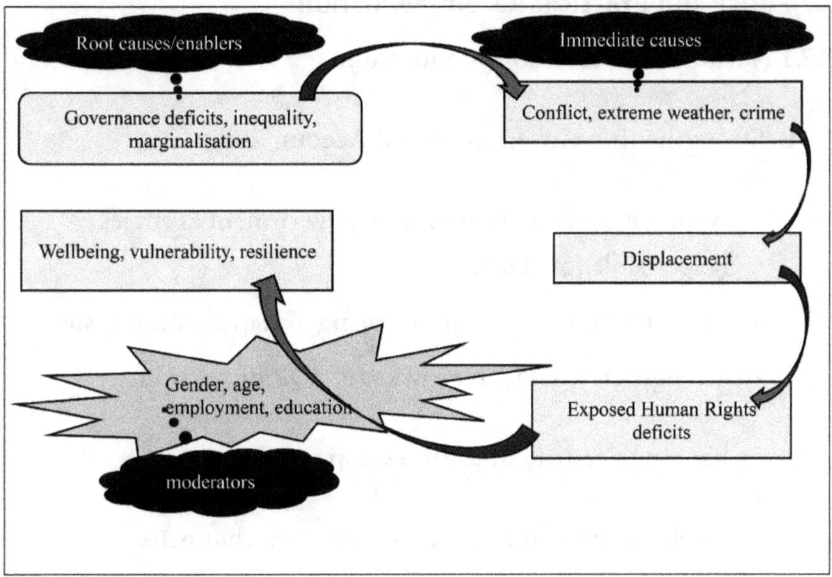

Figure 7.3 An Integrated African-centric Displacement and Human Rights Model

The three case studies covered in this book reveal that the causes of internal displacement are rooted in domestic factors, mainly governance deficits, poor service delivery, inequality and marginalization. These are the breeding grounds for conflict, crime, and poor planning in response to extreme weather events. Hence, displacement becomes inevitable in such unfortunate events. The hasty, unplanned and uncoordinated displacement of a large number of people exposes any human rights gaps that exist in the country. This study has also revealed that demographic factors, such as gender, age, employment status and education moderate the vulnerability and resilience of IDPs to Human Rights deficits. Women, for example, tend to be more exposed to Human Rights abuses than men.

7.7 Policy and Practical Recommendations

7.7.1 National-Level Recommendations

1. Strengthening Governance and Accountability

    - Improve coordination among government agencies responsible for IDPs.
    - Establish transparent monitoring and evaluation systems.
    - Strengthen legal frameworks for IDP protection.

2. Enhancing Security and Protection

    - Deploy community-based security mechanisms.
    - Improve policing and justice systems.
    - Address root causes of conflict and crime.

3. Expanding Access to Basic Services

    - Ensure equitable access to food, water, healthcare, and education.
    - Prioritize IDPs in national development plans.
    - Strengthen infrastructure in displacement-affected areas.

4. Promoting Economic Inclusion

    - Create livelihood programs and employment opportunities.
    - Support small businesses and informal sector activities.
    - Provide skills training and education.

5. Supporting Psychosocial and Community Recovery

    - Provide mental health services.
    - Promote family reunification and social cohesion.
    - Strengthen community-based support systems.

7.7.2 Country-Specific Priorities

Cameroon

- Address political grievances and promote inclusive governance.
- Strengthen peacebuilding and conflict resolution mechanisms.

South Africa

- Integrate climate adaptation with urban planning.
- Improve disaster preparedness and housing delivery.

Nigeria

- Enhance security and counter-insurgency strategies.
- Address ethno-religious tensions and resource conflicts.

7.7.3 Regional (Sub-Saharan Africa) Recommendations

1. Strengthening Implementation of the Kampala Convention

    - Improve national domestication and enforcement.
    - Enhance regional monitoring mechanisms.

2. Promoting Regional Cooperation
    - Share best practices across countries.
    - Strengthen cross-border humanitarian coordination.
3. Integrating Climate and Conflict Responses
    - Develop comprehensive frameworks addressing both environmental and conflict-related displacement.
4. Data and Research Strengthening
    - Improve data collection on IDPs, particularly those outside camps.
    - Support longitudinal and comparative research.
5. Financing and Partnerships
    - Increase investment in IDP protection and integration.
    - Strengthen partnerships between governments, NGOs, and international organizations.

7.8 Conclusion

This comparative analysis demonstrates that internal displacement in Africa is a complex and systemic human rights challenge that transcends national boundaries. While the specific drivers of displacement vary across Cameroon, South Africa, and Nigeria, the underlying patterns of inequality, insecurity, and governance deficits are remarkably similar.

Addressing these challenges requires integrated, rights-based, and context-sensitive approaches that prioritize both immediate humanitarian needs and long-term structural transformation.

Ultimately, improving the human rights conditions of internally displaced persons is not only a moral imperative but also a critical step toward achieving sustainable development and social justice in Africa.

CHAPTER 8

Human Rights of Internally Displaced Persons Information Is the Master Key to Protection and Support

Abstract

The empirical findings reported in this book reveal the gravity of the internal displacement situation within the borders of the affected countries and the Sub-Saharan African region in general and equally signal an urgent call to action in order to alleviate the level of distress on affected families and communities. The purpose of this final chapter is to draw attention to existing institutions and mechanisms that are available in selected countries and internationally to render assistance to internally displaced persons. While international frameworks, such as the United Nations Guiding Principles on Internal Displacement (1998) and the Universal Declaration of Human Rights (1948), provide the foundational prescripts for the protection of internally displaced persons, regional frameworks contextualize the policy guidelines that national laws and institutions implement at the community level. The chapter concludes with guidance on avenues where IDPs in Cameroon, Nigeria, and South Africa can access support and protection and legal assistance for refugees.

Key words: protection of IDPs, Human Rights, assistance, frameworks, institutions, legal aid.

8.1 Introduction

It is important for people who find themselves in situations of internal displacement or as refugees to understand that they are not to blame for their predicament. Nobody is responsible for the circumstances of their birth, be it nationality, geographic location, social class, political systems, gender, or even family affiliation. It might seem convenient to attribute blame to an individual or group of people for some of the decisions they made, but deeper reflections could lead us to question the wisdom of judging rather than asking more exploratory questions. Therefore, displaced persons are encouraged to familiarize themselves with their rights and entitlements and where to get access to protection and assistance.

8.2 Delimitations

It is important that certain boundaries are set and acknowledgements made in this book, primarily because of the fluidity and dynamic nature of the displacement concept. The number of displaced persons in any location is influenced by two phenomena: the number of new arrivals and the number of people who return to their homes or migrate to new locations. Therefore, the needs analysis of IDPs varies and changes periodically. Moreover, the range of services offered by the organizations is subject to change. The information provided here should be seen as a guide to other sources. Additionally, restricting the case studies discussed here to Cameroon, Nigeria, and South Africa was informed mainly by the need to illustrate the diverse causes of displacement in Sub-Saharan Africa and does not seek to undermine the internal displacement situation in other countries in the region.

7.3 Know Your Rights as an IDP

The theory of human rights has its roots in the critical writings of John Locke (1689), who emphasized the innate and inalienable rights of all human beings by virtue of their humanity. Locke (1689) referred to these as "natural rights" because they reflect the fact that human beings are rational creatures, capable of thinking for themselves, and pursuing happiness within the limits of natural laws (Frankle 1974). However, Locke (1689) argued that even though rational individuals will cede some of their rights to political authorities who will, in turn, be responsible for protecting the individual's natural rights, he insisted that individuals should always retain their natural rights to life, liberty, and property (Heyman 2018).

In Myer's (2017) view, the concept of human rights has changed significantly over the past few decades since the United Nations Declaration of Human Rights (UN 1948), where thirty articles with multiple accompanying proclaimed rights were endorsed by members of the global body.

Key legal instruments and frameworks at the global, regional, and national levels provide protection for internally displaced persons and, in some cases, refugees.

Major international frameworks guiding the protection of internally displaced persons:

United Nations Guiding Principles on Internal Displacement (1998)

Key Provisions: The United Nations Guiding Principles on Internal Displacement (1998) provide a comprehensive, non-binding international framework for protecting and assisting internally displaced persons (IDPs). These principles clarify the rights of IDPs and the responsibilities of states and other actors. Although they are not legally binding, they reflect and build upon existing international human rights law, humanitarian law, and refugee law by analogy.

Definition (Who is an IDP?): An Internally Displaced Person (IDP) is a person who has been forced or obliged to flee from their home and place of permanent residence due to:

- Armed conflict.
- Generalised violence.
- Human rights violations.
- Natural or human-made disasters.

Unlike refugees, IDPs have not crossed an international border.

International Protection and Rights (What protection and rights do IDPs have under international law?). There are thirty principles, grouped into five broad sections. Some (selected) protected rights of IDPs of direct significance to this book are summarised below:

I. General Principles (Principles 1-4)

Principle 1: IDPs have the same rights and freedoms as other persons in their country.

Principle 2: These principles apply to all IDPs, regardless of legal status.

Principle 3: National authorities have the primary duty to protect and assist IDPs.

Principle 4: Certain groups (children, the elderly, the disabled, and pregnant women) require special protection.

II. Protection from Displacement (Principles 5-8)

Principle 5: Arbitrary displacement is prohibited (e.g., for discriminatory or collective punishment reasons).

Principle 6: Displacement must be lawful, necessary, and involve consultation and safeguards.

Principle 7: Displacement should not be used to separate families.

Principle 8: States must take measures to prevent and mitigate displacement.

III. Protection During Displacement (Principles 10–23)

Covers a wide range of civil, political, economic, social, and cultural rights:

Life and Safety

Principle 10: IDPs have the right to life and protection from violence, including from military attacks and landmines.

Principle 11: Protection from torture, inhuman treatment, and gender-based violence.

Freedom of Movement and Family Life

Principle 14: Freedom of movement and residence within their country.

Principle 17: Protection of family unity and facilitation of reunification.

Access to Basic Needs

Principles 18–19: Right to food, water, shelter, health care, and sanitation.

Principle 20: Access to education, employment, and participation in public affairs.

Legal Identity and Documentation

Principle 21: States must issue or replace legal documents (e.g., birth certificates, IDs) without discrimination.

IV. Humanitarian Assistance (Principles 24-27)

Principle 24: Humanitarian assistance should be provided based on need alone, without discrimination.

Principle 25: National authorities bear primary responsibility but must allow international aid when needed.

Principle 26: IDPs have the right to freedom of association and to seek assistance collectively.

Principle 27: Protection must be ensured for humanitarian personnel and aid recipients.

V. Durable Solutions (Principles 28-30)

Principle 28: IDPs have the right to voluntarily return, integrate locally, or resettle elsewhere in safety and dignity.

Principle 29: States must assist in reintegration and ensure IDPs recover property and enjoy equal access to public services.

Principle 30: Duty to consult IDPs and involve them in decisions related to their future.

Legal Significance

The Guiding Principles are non-binding soft law, but they:

- Reflect and interpret binding norms of international law.

- Influence regional instruments, such as the African Union Convention for the Protection and Assistance of Internally Displaced Persons in Africa (Kampala Convention).
- Are widely used by governments, UN agencies, NGOs, and courts.

Universal Declaration of Human Rights (1948)

Another important international instrument or framework for the protection and support of internally displaced persons is the Universal Declaration of Human Rights (UDHR). The Universal Declaration of Human Rights (UDHR), adopted by the United Nations General Assembly in 1948, is a foundational document affirming the inherent dignity and equal rights of all human beings. It consists of thirty articles outlining a broad range of civil, political, economic, social, and cultural rights.

Key Principles and Prescripts of the UDHR (1948)

1. Equality and Non-Discrimination

    - Article 1: All human beings are born free and equal in dignity and rights.
    - Article 2: Rights apply to everyone without discrimination based on race, color, sex, language, religion, political opinion, national or social origin, birth, or other status.

2. Civil and Political Rights

    - Right to life, liberty, and security. (Art. 3)
    - Freedom from slavery. (Art. 4)

- Freedom from torture and inhuman treatment. (Art. 5)
- Recognition as a person before the law. (Art. 6)
- Equality before the law and right to legal remedy. (Arts. 7-8)
- Freedom from arbitrary arrest, detention, or exile. (Art. 9)
- Fair and public hearing by an independent tribunal. (Art. 10)
- Presumption of innocence until proven guilty. (Art. 11)

3. Freedoms of Expression, Religion, and Assembly

- Freedom of movement and residence within borders. (Art. 13)
- Right to seek asylum from persecution. (Art. 14)
- Right to nationality and change of nationality. (Art. 15)
- Freedom of thought, conscience, and religion. (Art. 18)
- Freedom of opinion and expression. (Art. 19)
- Right to peaceful assembly and association. (Art. 20)
- Right to participate in government and free elections. (Art. 21)

4. Economic, Social, and Cultural Rights

- Right to social security and economic rights. (Art. 22)
- Right to work, equal pay, and favorable conditions. (Art. 23)
- Right to rest and leisure (including paid holidays). (Art. 24)

- Right to adequate living standard (food, clothing, housing, health care). (Art. 25)
- Right to education. (Art. 26)
- Right to participate in cultural life and benefit from scientific advancement. (Art. 27)

5. Dignity, Family, and Protection

- Right to marry and found a family. (Art. 16)
- Right to privacy and protection of reputation. (Art. 12)
- Parents' Right to Choose Children's Education (Art. 26.3)

6. Duties and International Order

- Article 28: Right to a social and international order where rights can be fully realized.
- Article 29: Everyone has duties to the community; rights may be limited only by law for the general welfare.
- Article 30: No state, group, or person may engage in activity aimed at destroying any of the rights and freedoms in the UDHR.

Impact: The UDHR has inspired over seventy national constitutions and is the foundation for modern human rights law, including treaties, such as the International Covenant on Civil and Political Rights (ICCPR) and the International Covenant on Economic, Social, and Cultural Rights (ICESCR).

Regional Protection and Support (African Union support for IDPs)

The African Union Convention for the Protection and Assistance of Internally Displaced Persons in Africa, commonly known as the Kampala Convention, holds profound significance in the protection of internally displaced persons (IDPs) on the African continent. Adopted in 2009, it is the first legally binding regional instrument in the world that specifically addresses the rights and needs of IDPs. Its significance lies in its comprehensive and legally enforceable framework, which obligates African Union (AU) member states not only to protect and assist IDPs, but also to prevent the causes of displacement.

The convention recognizes a wide range of displacement drivers, including armed conflict, human rights violations, natural disasters, and development-induced displacement, such as infrastructure or extractive projects. It compels state parties to take concrete actions—from early warning systems and conflict prevention to the provision of humanitarian assistance and the facilitation of durable solutions like voluntary return, local integration, or relocation. Furthermore, the convention uniquely places responsibilities on non-state actors, including armed groups and private corporations, and calls for accountability and respect for the rights of displaced populations. It also highlights the particular vulnerabilities of women, children, the elderly, and persons with disabilities, requiring targeted protection measures.

In contrast, the United Nations Guiding Principles on Internal Displacement (1998) are non-binding, soft law instruments that serve as a moral and operational framework for the protection of IDPs globally. While highly influential and widely cited, the UN Guiding Principles do not carry the force of law and rely on voluntary adoption and implementation by states. The principles outline the rights of IDPs and the duties of national authorities but stop short of mandating enforcement or imposing legal obligations. The Kampala Convention builds on and localizes the UN Guiding Principles, incorporating their norms into a binding legal instrument tailored to the African context. This makes the Kampala Convention not only a regional endorsement of the UN principles but also a more actionable and enforceable mechanism for addressing internal displacement. Its legal force, regional specificity, and expanded scope—including the responsibilities of non-state actors—mark a significant evolution from the UN Guiding Principles and reflect Africa's proactive stance in confronting the continent's displacement crises.

Major Attributes of the Kampala Convention (What the Kampala Convention offers IDPs)

The African Union Convention for the Protection and Assistance of Internally Displaced Persons in Africa, also known as the Kampala Convention (2009), is the first legally binding regional instrument in the world that specifically addresses the protection and assistance of internally displaced persons (IDPs). Below are the key highlights of the Convention:

1. Obligations of countries that signed the Kampala Convention:

    - Prevent displacement through early warning, disaster preparedness, and conflict resolution.
    - Protect IDPs during displacement by respecting their rights (e.g., life, dignity, family unity, property).
    - Assist and support IDPs with food, shelter, health care, education, and documentation.
    - Promote durable solutions, including voluntary return, local integration, or resettlement in another part of the country.

2. Responsibilities beyond the state

    - Non-state actors, such as armed groups, also have duties not to cause displacement and to respect the rights of IDPs.
    - Private sector and multinational corporations must avoid activities (like resource extraction or infrastructure development) that cause unlawful displacement.

3. Protection from Arbitrary Displacement

    - Displacement should not be arbitrary or discriminatory.
    - States must consult affected communities and conduct impact assessments before any development-induced displacement.

4. Special Protection for Vulnerable Groups
   Emphasizes protection for:

    - Women and children.
    - Persons with disabilities.
    - Elderly persons.
    - Minority and indigenous communities.

5. Role of the African Union and Humanitarian Agencies

    - Encourages cooperation with the African Union, humanitarian organizations, and civil society in providing assistance and promoting durable solutions.

6. Monitoring and Accountability

    - States must adopt national legal frameworks and establish institutions for implementation.
    - Periodic reporting to the African Union on measures taken to fulfil obligations.

7. Durable Solutions and Post-Displacement Support

    - Ensures the voluntary and safe return of IDPs.
    - Requires restoration of housing, land, and property rights.
    - Promotes reintegration and reconstruction efforts.

The Kampala Convention represents a landmark in international and regional humanitarian law, offering a comprehensive approach to addressing internal displacement in Africa and placing legal responsibility on governments to prevent and respond to the needs of IDPs.

Case Studies on Protection Mechanisms and Help for Internally Displaced Persons in Cameroon, Nigeria, and South Africa

Cameroon Context

Legal and policy framework guiding the management of internal displacement in Cameroon.

Cameroon faces significant internal displacement due to conflict, violence (especially in the Far North, Northwest, and Southwest regions), natural disasters, and development projects. The country has taken steps—though still limited and evolving—to develop a framework for managing internal displacement and protecting the rights of internally displaced persons (IDPs).

Currently, there is no comprehensive national law specifically dedicated to the management of internal displacement in Cameroon. However, the country relies on a mix of international, regional, and domestic legal instruments to address IDP issues.

1. **The application of international and regional instruments:**

    - Kampala Convention (ratified in 2014): As a member state of the African Union, Cameroon is legally bound to the African Union Convention for the Protection and Assistance of Internally Displaced Persons in Africa (Kampala Convention). It mandates states to prevent displacement, protect and assist IDPs, and find durable solutions.
    - UN Guiding Principles on Internal Displacement: While non-binding, these principles are referenced in humanitarian operations and advocacy.

Knowledge of the laws protecting internally displaced persons is important, but it is equally important to know the institutions and organisations where IDPs can go for direct assistance.

Institutional mechanisms for the management of internal displacement in Cameroon

Here is a summary of key organizations and legal institutions offering assistance to internally displaced persons (IDPs) and refugees from Cameroon, both within the country and in regional or international contexts. These actors provide protection, humanitarian aid, legal support, and advocacy.

1. National and Local Institutions in Cameroon

   a. Ministry of Territorial Administration (MINAT)

   - Mandate: Coordinates civil protection and internal security and leads emergency response efforts.
   - Role for IDPs: Oversees displacement response, particularly through its Civil Protection Directorate.
   - Limitations: Often under-resourced and reactive rather than proactive.

   b. Civil Protection Directorate (under MINAT)

   - Coordinates disaster response, evacuation, and temporary shelters during crises, such as floods or conflict-induced displacement.

   c. Ministry of Social Affairs (MINAS)

   - Supports vulnerable populations, including IDPs and persons with disabilities.
   - Offers limited welfare support, including child protection and social reintegration services.

   d. Cameroon Human Rights Commission (CHRC)

   - National institution for monitoring and promoting human rights.
   - Receives complaints and investigates rights violations affecting IDPs and refugees.
   - Advocates for better protection mechanisms.

2. International and Regional Organizations

   a. United Nations High Commissioner for Refugees (UNHCR)

- Mandate: Protects refugees and assists IDPs in certain contexts.
- In Cameroon: Provides shelter, documentation, legal assistance, and advocacy for displaced persons in conflict regions (especially Northwest, Southwest, and Far North).
- Works closely with national authorities and other UN bodies.

   b. International Organization for Migration (IOM)

- Supports displacement tracking (DTM), shelter, health, and reintegration of IDPs.
- Works on peacebuilding and community stabilization programs.
- Active in the Lake Chad Basin crisis areas.

   c. United Nations Office for the Coordination of Humanitarian Affairs (OCHA)

- Coordinates the humanitarian response to internal displacement, including through cluster leadership (e.g., shelter, protection, education).
- Produces situation reports and appeals for international funding.

d. UNICEF

- Provides child protection, education, and health services for displaced children and families.
- Supports safe learning spaces and psychosocial support in displacement-affected communities.

e. World Food Programme (WFP)

- Delivers food aid and nutritional support to IDPs, especially in the Far North and Anglophone regions.

f. Médecins Sans Frontières (MSF) / Doctors Without Borders

- Offers medical and mental health support to displaced persons in conflict-affected areas.
- Has faced operational restrictions in parts of Cameroon due to conflict dynamics.

3. Local and International NGOs

a. Reach Out Cameroon

- Provides health, education, and livelihood support to displaced and vulnerable persons in the Southwest region.

b. Center for Human Rights and Democracy in Africa (CHRDA)

- Based in Buea, provides legal assistance, documents human rights abuses, and advocates for the rights of IDPs and other affected civilians.

c. Plan International

- Active in child protection, education, and gender-based violence prevention for displaced children and women.

d. Norwegian Refugee Council (NRC)

- Offers shelter, education, legal aid, and livelihood support to IDPs, especially in conflict-affected zones.

e. Catholic Relief Services (CRS) and Caritas Cameroon

- Provide emergency relief, housing, and psychosocial services to displaced communities.

4. Regional and Legal Mechanisms

a. African Commission on Human and Peoples' Rights (ACHPR)

- Monitors compliance with the African Charter and receives individual complaints of rights violations.
- Engages with Cameroon on implementation of the Kampala Convention on IDP protection.

b. Economic Community of Central African States (ECCAS)

- While not highly active in field response, ECCAS encourages regional cooperation on peace and displacement issues.

Where to Get Help in the United States

If you are a refugee from Cameroon and currently in the United States, several organizations provide free legal support and immigration assistance, including for asylum applications, work permits, and deportation defense. Here are trusted resources you can contact:

Free Legal Services for Refugees from Cameroon

1. Refugee and Immigrant Center for Education and Legal Services (RAICES)

   - Services: Asylum applications, bond assistance, legal representation in immigration court.
   - Website: https://www.raicestexas.org
   - Location: Based in Texas but supports clients nationally.

2. Catholic Charities Immigration Legal Services

   - Services: Asylum, Temporary Protected Status (TPS), family petitions, work authorization.
   - Offices: Available in many states (e.g., New York, DC, Chicago, Los Angeles).
   - Website: https://www.catholiccharitiesusa.org

3. African Communities Together (ACT)

   - Services: Legal aid, advocacy, and empowerment for African immigrants, including Cameroonians.
   - Location: Offices in New York, Washington D.C., and beyond.
   - Website: https://www.africans.us

4. The International Refugee Assistance Project (IRAP)

   - Services: Legal representation for refugees and displaced persons seeking protection in the U.S.
   - Website: https://refugeerights.org

5. American Immigration Lawyers Association (AILA) – Pro Bono Services

   - Services: Can help match you with a volunteer immigration attorney.
   - Directory: https://www.aila.org

6. National Immigration Legal Services Directory (Immigration Advocates Network)

   - Tool: Find free or low-cost immigration legal services by ZIP code.
   - Search Tool: https://www.immigrationadvocates.org/legaldirectory

Key Services to Ask For

When contacting these organizations, ask if they can help you with:

- Filing for asylum or defensive asylum in immigration court.
- Applying for work authorization (EAD).
- Understanding if you qualify for TPS (Cameroon is currently designated).
- Removal defence or ICE-related concerns.
- Assistance with refugee resettlement services or benefits.

Nigerian Context

Framework for Managing Internal Displacement in Nigeria

Nigeria faces one of the highest rates of internal displacement in Africa, primarily due to armed conflict (e.g., Boko Haram insurgency), farmer-herder clashes, banditry, natural disasters, and development-induced displacement. The country has developed a patchwork framework for managing internal displacement, combining national, regional, and international instruments—but critical gaps remain in legal codification, coordination, and durable solutions.

1. Legal and Policy Frameworks

   a. Absence of a Dedicated National IDP Law
   Nigeria does not yet have a comprehensive national legal

framework specifically focused on internal displacement. However, efforts have been made toward this:

- Draft National Policy on Internally Displaced Persons (IDPs) (2012, revised in 2021): Provides guiding principles for prevention, protection, assistance, and durable solutions for IDPs. Though approved by the Federal Executive Council in 2021, it is not legally binding unless enacted into law by the National Assembly.

b. International and Regional Instruments

- Kampala Convention: Nigeria was the first African country to domesticate the African Union Convention on the Protection and Assistance of Internally Displaced Persons (2012).
- UN Guiding Principles on Internal Displacement: Serve as a non-binding framework influencing national policy and humanitarian practice.

c. Constitutional Rights

- The 1999 Nigerian Constitution (as amended) guarantees fundamental human rights, including protection of life, dignity, and freedom of movement, applicable to IDPs.

2. Institutional Framework

a. National Emergency Management Agency (NEMA): Established in 1999, NEMA is the lead government agency for coordinating responses to displacement and disasters.

It works with state emergency management agencies (SEMAs), but capacity varies greatly.

b. National Commission for Refugees, Migrants, and Internally Displaced Persons (NCFRMI): Tasked with policy formulation, data collection, protection, and coordination of durable solutions. NCFRMI has a broader mandate than NEMA, but coordination is often fragmented.

c. State-Level Involvement: SEMAs, state ministries, and local governments are expected to play active roles but often lack adequate funding, training, and infrastructure.

d. Humanitarian Coordination: International actors, such as UNHCR, IOM, OCHA, and INGOs, support the response, particularly in Northeast Nigeria. Coordination is organized through sectoral clusters (e.g., health, protection, education, shelter).

3. Protection and Assistance Mechanisms

a. Humanitarian Assistance

- IDPs are housed in both formal camps and host communities, particularly in the Northeast.
- Services provided include food distribution, medical care, water and sanitation, education, and psychosocial support.
- Assistance is often inadequate, and some camps are overcrowded and underfunded.

b. Protection Concerns

- IDPs face violations of rights, including sexual and gender-based violence (SGBV), child labor, human trafficking, and lack of access to identity documents.
- Security forces, vigilante groups, and camp managers have been implicated in abuses.

c. Durable Solutions

- Local integration, return, and relocation are the three options considered, but implementation is weak.
- Involuntary returns and premature camp closures, especially in Borno State, have raised concerns about safety and sustainability.

4. Key Challenges and Gaps

- No enforceable IDP law: The national policy lacks legislative backing.
- Weak institutional coordination: NEMA and NCFRMI often operate in silos; SEMAs lack resources.
- Funding shortages: Humanitarian response relies heavily on international donors.
- Data issues: Lack of accurate, real-time data on IDP numbers and needs.
- Limited IDP participation: Displaced persons are rarely involved in decisions affecting their futures.

5. Recommendations for Strengthening the Framework

- Enact the National IDP Policy into law to provide a binding legal framework.
- Strengthen inter-agency coordination, including clear mandates for NEMA, NCFRMI, and SEMAs.
- Build state-level capacity for IDP response and durable solution planning.
- Enhance protection mechanisms, especially for women, children, and persons with disabilities.
- Promote inclusive, durable solutions guided by IDP preferences and safety considerations.

Conclusion

Nigeria's current framework for managing internal displacement is evolving but fragmented. While the country has taken important steps, particularly by domesticating the Kampala Convention, the lack of a binding national law and weak institutional coordination hinder effective protection and durable solutions. Strengthening legal frameworks and institutional capacity at all levels remains essential for addressing Nigeria's complex displacement crisis.

Help Is Available

Here is a summary of key organizations and legal institutions offering assistance to internally displaced persons (IDPs) and refugees from Nigeria, both within Nigeria and abroad, including in host countries where Nigerian refugees have sought asylum (such as Cameroon, Niger, and the United States).

1. National Institutions and Legal Bodies in Nigeria

a. National Commission for Refugees, Migrants and Internally Displaced Persons (NCFRMI)

- Mandate: Government agency responsible for coordinating IDP and refugee protection, reintegration, and durable solutions.
- Services: Registration, assistance coordination, reintegration planning, data management.
- Website: https://ncfrmi.gov.ng

b. National Emergency Management Agency (NEMA)

- Mandate: Coordinates emergency responses to displacement caused by conflict, natural disasters, and other crises.
- Role: Works with State Emergency Management Agencies (SEMAs) to provide relief items, temporary shelter, and support during emergencies.

c. National Human Rights Commission (NHRC)

- Mandate: Promotes and protects human rights in Nigeria, including the rights of displaced persons.
- Services: Receives complaints of abuse, conducts investigations, and provides legal advocacy.

2. International and Regional Organizations in Nigeria

a. United Nations High Commissioner for Refugees (UNHCR)

- Mandate: Protects refugees, returnees, asylum seekers, and stateless persons.
- In Nigeria: Supports displaced persons in the Northeast and Nigerian refugees returning from neighboring countries.
- Website: https://www.unhcr.org/ng

b. International Organization for Migration (IOM)

- Role: Provides emergency shelter, psychosocial support, data tracking (DTM), livelihood programs, and reintegration assistance.
- Website: https://nigeria.iom.int

c. United Nations Children's Fund (UNICEF)

- Focus: Assists displaced children and families with education, water and sanitation, nutrition, and child protection.

d. World Food Programme (WFP)

- Services: Food distribution and nutrition support for IDPs in the Northeast and food-insecure communities.

e. International Committee of the Red Cross (ICRC) & Nigerian Red Cross Society

- Mandate: Offers humanitarian aid, family reunification, healthcare, and protection to people affected by conflict and displacement.

3. Local and International NGOs in Nigeria

a. Norwegian Refugee Council (NRC)

- Services: Legal aid, education, shelter, and livelihood support to displaced communities.
- Special Focus: Housing, land, and property rights for IDPs.

b. Catholic Relief Services (CRS) and Caritas Nigeria

- Provide humanitarian assistance, including food, shelter, and psychosocial support in IDP-hosting communities.

c. Mercy Corps, Action Against Hunger (AAH), and Save the Children

- Implement health, education, food security, and child protection programs in displacement-affected areas.

d. Center for Democracy and Development (CDD)

- Advocates for IDP rights, conducts policy research, and supports community reconciliation and peacebuilding.

4. International Support for Nigerian Refugees Abroad

a. UNHCR (in Cameroon, Niger, Chad, Benin)

- Services: Refugee status determination, legal assistance, shelter, health care, and resettlement support for Nigerian refugees.
- Focus Areas: Cross-border protection from Boko Haram and other conflicts.

b. Jesuit Refugee Service (JRS)

- Active in Cameroon and Chad, offering legal aid, education, psychosocial services, and advocacy for Nigerian refugees.

c. Cameroon Red Cross, Niger Red Cross, Chad Red Cross

- Provide humanitarian assistance to Nigerian refugee populations and IDPs in border regions.

5. Legal Assistance for Nigerian Refugees in the United States

For Nigerian refugees and asylum seekers in the U.S., the following organizations offer free or low-cost immigration legal services:

Organisation	Services
RAICES	Asylum, work permit, court defence (raicestexas.org)
African Communities Together (ACT)	Legal aid and advocacy for African immigrants (africans.us)
Catholic Charities	Asylum, TPS, family petitions, and legal representation

International Refugee Assistance Project (IRAP)	Legal help with refugee claims and resettlement
Immigration Advocates Network	Search for local legal help

Conclusion

Nigeria's framework for managing displacement involves a network of national agencies, international bodies, and civil society organizations. While these entities provide critical services, challenges persist in legal protection, durable solutions, and resource limitations. For refugees outside Nigeria, UNHCR and NGOs continue to offer assistance, but access and adequacy vary by host country.

South African Context

Framework for Managing Internal Displacement in South Africa

Unlike many African countries facing conflict-related displacement, internal displacement in South Africa is driven mainly by natural disasters, xenophobic violence, forced evictions, and urban development projects. South Africa does not officially recognize or categorize persons displaced internally as "IDPs" in the formal sense, and thus has no dedicated legal or policy framework specifically addressing internal displacement. Nevertheless, several constitutional guarantees, sectoral laws, and disaster management systems provide indirect protection and assistance.

Constitutional Protections

The 1996 Constitution provides strong protection for all people in South Africa, including:

- Section 26: Right to adequate housing and protection against arbitrary evictions.
- Section 27: Right to health care, food, water, and social security.
- Section 9: Right to equality and protection from discrimination.

These provisions apply to displaced persons regardless of legal classification.

Applicable Sectoral Laws

- Prevention of Illegal Eviction from and Unlawful Occupation of Land Act (PIE Act) (1998): Protects against forced evictions without due process.
- Disaster Management Act (2002): Provides the framework for responding to natural disasters and emergencies, including temporary resettlement.
- Housing Act (1997) and Emergency Housing Programme: Allow for temporary housing assistance after displacement caused by fires, floods, or evictions.

Displacement Context and Assistance Mechanisms

a. Disaster-Induced Displacement: Common in urban informal settlements due to flooding, fires, and storms. Temporary shelter is often provided via municipal emergency housing grants, but responses are frequently delayed and under-resourced.

b. Violence-Induced Displacement: Xenophobic attacks (e.g., 2008, 2015, 2019) have caused mass displacement of foreign nationals and some South Africans. Temporary shelters were established but often lacked long-term solutions or reintegration planning.

c. Forced Evictions and Development Displacement: Urban upgrades, evictions from informal settlements, and land clearance for infrastructure projects regularly result in displacement, often without adequate consultation or relocation support.

Where to Get Help as an IDP in South Africa

1. National and Local Institutions in South Africa

   a. Department of Home Affairs (DHA)

   - Mandate: Handles refugee and asylum seeker documentation under the Refugees Act (1998) and Immigration Act (2002).
   - Services:
     - Asylum seeker permits and refugee status determination.
     - Regulation of refugee reception centers.
   - Challenges: Long delays, access issues, and administrative backlogs are common.

b. Department of Human Settlements (DHS)

- Role: Provides emergency housing and coordinates relocation for people displaced by evictions, informal settlement fires, and floods.

c. South African Human Rights Commission (SAHRC)

- Mandate: Monitors human rights abuses and provides legal advice, especially for xenophobic violence survivors, displaced migrants, and evicted communities.
- Services:
    - Investigating human rights complaints.
    - Advocacy and public education.
    - Emergency interventions during displacement crises.

2. International and Regional Organizations Active in South Africa

a. United Nations High Commissioner for Refugees (UNHCR)

- Mandate: Provides protection, advocacy, and services for refugees and asylum seekers in South Africa (mostly from other African countries).
- Services:
    - Legal aid through partner NGOs.

    - Psychosocial support, livelihood programs, and community integration.
    - Website: https://www.unhcr.org/za

b. International Organization for Migration (IOM)

- Mandate: Assists migrants and displaced persons, including return and reintegration for victims of trafficking and stranded migrants.
- In South Africa:

    - Offers voluntary return and reintegration assistance.
    - Helps communities recover from displacement and reintegrate migrants.

c. Médecins Sans Frontières (MSF)

- Offers healthcare and mental health services to vulnerable displaced groups in informal settlements and migrant communities, especially during crisis events.

3. NGOs and Legal Aid Organizations in South Africa

a. Lawyers for Human Rights (LHR)

- One of the leading providers of legal support to asylum seekers, refugees, and displaced people.
- Services:

    - Legal representation in asylum/refugee appeals.

- Assistance with documentation, detention monitoring, and statelessness cases.
- Website: https://www.lhr.org.za

b. Refugee Legal and Advocacy Center (RLAC)

- Provides legal advice and representation to asylum seekers and recognized refugees, especially in Johannesburg and Pretoria.

c. Scalabrini Center of Cape Town

- Focus: Migrants, refugees, and displaced people.
- Services:
    - Legal aid.
    - English and computer literacy.
    - Refugee rights education.
    - Website: https://www.scalabrini.org.za

d. Center for Applied Legal Studies (CALS) – University of the Witwatersrand

- Offers legal research, litigation, and advocacy on housing, evictions, and displacement.
- Actively supports displaced communities and fights for access to shelter and services.

e. Consortium for Refugees and Migrants in South Africa (CoRMSA)

- A coalition of NGOs working on refugee rights, anti-xenophobia campaigns, and migration policy reform.
- Offers advocacy and coordination among legal aid providers.

4. Displacement Scenarios in South Africa

Causes of displacement	Affected group	Support mechanism
Xenophobic violence	Foreign refugees, migrants	UNHCR, SAHRC, LHR, Scalabrini, MSF
Evictions/informal settlement clearance	Previously disadvantaged and poor South African citizens	DHS, SAHRC, CALS
Displacement due to insecurity or unrest	Refugees and asylum seekers	UNHCR, LHR, CoRMSA

Conclusion

South Africa has a strong constitutional and legal foundation for protecting displaced persons, but implementation remains uneven, and there is no dedicated IDP legal framework. Refugees (mostly from other African countries) and vulnerable South Africans facing eviction or violence rely heavily on NGOs, international agencies, and advocacy bodies for legal assistance and humanitarian support.

REFERENCES

Acha-Anyi, P. N. (2023). A tale of five cities: Residents' perceptions of the African Cup of Nations tournament in Cameroon. GeoJournal of Tourism and Geosites, 49(3), 1096–1108. https://doi.org/10.30892/gtg.49325-1109

Acha-Anyi, P. N. (2024). Unmasking the human rights needs of internally displaced persons: A case study of selected states in Nigeria. International Journal of Migration, Health and Social Care, 20(4), 682–700. https://doi.org/10.1108/ijmhsc-02-2023-0016

Adeola, R. (2020). The internally displaced persons in Africa: Law and policy in the African Union. Routledge.

Adeola, R. (2021). National protection of internally displaced persons in Africa: Beyond the rhetoric. Springer.

Ademola, E. O. (2020). Herder-farmer conflicts and RUGA policy. Ethnic Studies Review, 43(3), 103–121. https://doi.org/10.1525/esr.2020.43.3.103

Adenuga, G. A. (2022). The indigeneity clause and ethnic diversity in Nigeria. Dynamics of Politics and Democracy, 1(2), 97–107.

Adenuga, G., Adenuga, A., & Oderinde, O. (2022). Intra-party conflicts and party stability in Nigeria. Annals of Management and Organization Research, 3(2), 141–151.

Adenuga, G., Olajubu, A., Oyewole, S., & Omotola, J. S. (2023). Ethno-religious conflicts in Nigeria. South African Review of Sociology, 53(2), 130–149.

Ager, A., & Ager, J. (2011). Faith, secularism, and humanitarian engagement. Journal of Refugee Studies, 24(3), 456–472.

African Commission on Human and Peoples' Rights. (2024). Resolution on forced internal displacement (ACHPR.Res. 582).

African Risk Capacity. (2024). The state of natural disasters in Africa. https://www.arc.int

African Union. (1981). African Charter on Human and Peoples' Rights.

African Union. (2009). Kampala Convention.

African Union. (2012). Convention for the protection and assistance of internally displaced persons in Africa.

African Union. (2019). Africa humanitarian report.

Ali, A. M. A., et al. (2024). Health problems among internally displaced persons in Sudan. BMC Public Health, 24(1). https://doi.org/10.1186/s12889-024-20972-1

Amnesty International. (2022). Amnesty International report 2021/2022: The state of the world's human rights.

Amnesty International. (2023). South Africa: Addressing displaced women and children.

Anierobi, C. M., et al. (2024). Communal conflicts in Nigeria. Heliyon. https://doi.org/10.1016/j.heliyon.2024.e30200

Autesserre, S. (2010). The trouble with the Congo. Cambridge University Press.

Bang, H. N., & Balgah, R. A. (2022). Cameroon's Anglophone crisis. Journal of International Humanitarian Action, 7(6).

Boeyink, C., et al. (2022). Pathways to care for IDPs. Journal of Migration and Health, 6, 100129.

Cernea, M. M. (2000). Risks and reconstruction in displacement. Economic and Political Weekly, 35(41), 3659–3678.

Cohen, R., & Deng, F. M. (1998). Masses in flight. Brookings Institution Press.

Creswell, J. W., & Plano Clark, V. L. (2018). Designing and conducting mixed methods research (3rd ed.). SAGE.

Dahie, H. A., et al. (2023). Gender-based violence among IDPs. Journal of Migration and Health, 8, 100193.

Dirikgil, N. (2022). Prevention of internal displacement. Journal of International Migration and Integration.

Ferris, E. (2011). Faith and humanitarianism. Brookings Institution.

Frankle, R. J. (1974). Declaration of rights. The Historical Journal, 17(2), 265–279.

Galtung, J. (1969). Violence, peace, and peace research. Journal of Peace Research, 6(3), 167–191.

Girum Nakie, et al. (2025). Depression among IDPs in Africa. BMC Psychiatry, 25(1).

Holloway, A. (2017). Disaster risk management in Southern Africa. University of Cape Town Press.

Horowitz, D. L. (1985). Ethnic groups in conflict. University of California Press.

Internal Displacement Monitoring Centre. (2024). Global report on internal displacement.

Internal Displacement Monitoring Centre. (2025). Global report on internal displacement.

Intergovernmental Panel on Climate Change. (2022). Climate change 2022.

International Organization for Migration. (2017). Framework for addressing internal displacement.

International Organization for Migration. (2024). World migration report 2024.

Kälin, W. (2008). Guiding principles on internal displacement.

Krejcie, R. V., & Morgan, D. W. (1970). Sample size determination. Educational and Psychological Measurement, 30(3), 607–610.

Levitt, P. (2007). God needs no passport. New Press.

Locke, J. (1948). Second treatise of government. Blackwell.

Marrus, M. R. (1985). The unwanted. Oxford University Press.

Mateko, F. M., & Vutula, N. (2024). Disaster-induced displacement. Natural Hazards.

Maxwell, D., et al. (2016). Facing famine in Somalia. Oxford University Press.

Metz, T. (2011). Ubuntu as a moral theory. African Human Rights Law Journal, 11(2), 532–559.

Myers, P. C. (2017). From natural rights to human rights.

Ndlovu-Gatsheni, S. J. (2013). Coloniality of power in Africa.

Nussbaum, M. (2011). Creating capabilities. Harvard University Press.

Office for the Coordination of Humanitarian Affairs. (2024). Sudan humanitarian update.

OHCHR. (2006). Human rights-based approach to development cooperation.

Okafor, O. C. (2007). The African human rights system. Cambridge University Press.

Posner, E. A. (2026). Human rights and development. World Bank.

Rodney, W. (1972). How Europe underdeveloped Africa.

Sarfaty, G. A. (2012). Values in translation. Stanford University Press.

Schlosberg, D. (2012). Climate justice. Environmental Politics.

Sen, A. (1999). Development as freedom. Oxford University Press.

Stockholm International Peace Research Institute. (2024). Armed conflict in sub-Saharan Africa.

Swartz, J., et al. (2023). Health and internal displacement. Journal of Migration and Health.

Tamale, S. (2020). Decolonization and Afro-feminism.

United Nations. (1948). Universal Declaration of Human Rights.

United Nations. (1951). Convention relating to the status of refugees.

United Nations. (1966a). International Covenant on Civil and Political Rights.

United Nations. (1966b). International Covenant on Economic, Social and Cultural Rights.

United Nations. (1998). Guiding principles on internal displacement.

United Nations Development Programme. (1994). Human development report.

United Nations Development Programme. (2017). Famine response report.

Von Uexkull, N., & Pettersson, T. (2018). African nonstate conflicts. International Interactions, 44(5), 953–968.

Watson, D. C. (2023). Inter-communal violence in Africa. Civil Wars.

World Bank. (2017). Country partnership framework for Cameroon.

Zolberg, A. R., Suhrke, A., & Aguayo, S. (1989). Escape from violence. Oxford University Press.

www.ingramcontent.com/pod-product-compliance
Lightning Source LLC
LaVergne TN
LVHW010838120826
845149LV00017B/3155

9798995770008